FITNESS FOR HORSE & RIDER

FITNESS FOR HORSE & RIDER

Gain more from your riding by improving your horse's fitness and condition — and your own

JANE HOLDERNESS-RODDAM

Photographs by Bob Langrish

David & Charles

IN APPRECIATION

The original synopsis for the book was written by the late Mrs Peggoty Henriques, whose untimely death robbed the horse world not only of a great personality but also one who contributed so much towards the riding and dressage world in particular.

I have tried to retain her original, sound ideas, putting my own interpretation on what I believe were her thoughts on how to be fit and able to enjoy horses and riding to the full.

All of us in the horse world miss her greatly.

Photographs by Bob Langrish

A DAVID & CHARLES BOOK

Copyright © Jane Holderness-Roddam 1993
First published 1993

Jane Holderness-Roddam has asserted her right to be
identified as author of this work in accordance with the
Copyright, Designs and Patents Act 1988.

A catalogue record for this book is available from the British Library.

ISBN 0 7153 9995 0

Typeset in 10/12½ pt Aster by ICON Graphic Services, Exeter
and printed in Italy by Milanostampa SpA
for David & Charles
Brunel House   Newton Abbot   Devon

CONTENTS

INTRODUCTION

Fitness can be described as a state of health whereby the person or animal is in a suitable condition, and adequately trained and ready to achieve whatever is asked; this takes a certain amount of work, time and effort depending on the degree of fitness required. To enjoy anything in life a certain basic fitness is necessary, whether you are on a horse preparing for a big competition, or only going for walks in the countryside. At some stage, however, those who ride or are thinking of taking it up will gain maximum benefit and be able to achieve much more if they are properly prepared through a gradually progressive routine – thus ultimate goals may be accomplished with relative physical ease.

This book is aimed more for the weekend rider or one-horse owner who does not have the time or the opportunity to ride regularly, rather than for those who ride several horses daily which is perhaps the ideal way of building up riding fitness. It is perfectly possible, however, to reach the necessary degree of fitness by knowing and understanding the basic requirements and adapting these to suit your lifestyle. With positive thinking and a bit of determined dedication, the enjoyment of preparing yourself and your horse, and succeeding in whichever of the equestrian activities you choose, is there for the taking: the following pages are aimed at helping you towards your goal.

I was extremely fortunate to be chosen to ride in the three-day event team at the Mexico Olympics whilst training as a nurse at the

Middlesex Hospital in London. In a sport such as eventing, fitness is vital for both horse and rider, and while I was lucky enough to be able to rely on my sister Jennie Loriston-Clarke to keep Our Nobby on target, I made sure I could ride four times a week by planning riding times round my nursing rota, even though it required driving ninety miles to the New Forest and back to do so! Even night duty could be coped with, by a change in my sleep routine. I would come off duty at eight in the morning and drive straight down to ride, then sleep for three hours and go back to London where I would sleep for another hour and go back on duty. I would then sleep really well the next day, and do the same thing – drive down and ride – the day after! Nowadays with shorter working hours it would probably be possible to have ridden two days running and then enjoy a good sleep.

Using the stairs instead of the lift in the hospital and nursing home, and skipping on the roof (building up to eight hundred skips three times a week) ensured I was just as fit

as anyone else. Once selected I added swimming and running to my routine on the days I could not ride, as the altitude and heat were to be an added problem.

I am a great believer that most things are achievable with a bit of planning and thought, so long as it is a realistic goal in the first place. Depending on what it is that you are aiming for, it may be necessary to allow extra time to achieve fitness or to ask a friend to help you out with the riding. See if you can arrange say, the extra hour required by coming in an hour earlier or later to work and make this up somewhere else in the day. In many jobs flexible working hours are possible, and numerous people have found ingenious ways to combine work with pleasure – this has been fun for all those involved as well as an inspiration to others wondering how to cope.

Whether you have your own horse or not, one of the first things to think about is what you are really aiming to achieve from riding. It is a fairly expensive hobby, as well as being time-consuming if you keep your horse at home. If you are not particularly ambitious, hacking or trekking in lovely surroundings may be all you want to do; once you can ride, the build-up of fitness for this is not too difficult.

Other people want to do more, such as pleasure riding leading on to endurance rides – for this both horse and rider will need a careful build-up to peak fitness if a successful outcome is to be achieved. There are, of course, competitions of all kinds for the really ambitious.

This book is divided into three parts, covering various stages in rider fitness as well as that of the horse, with useful advice for all at the end. In Part One the complete beginner is considered, and the information may also be useful to those who have not ridden for some years and are thinking of taking it up again. While not in any way intended as a 'learn-to-ride' book, the basics of riding are discussed in such a way that the reader will be able to avoid many of the pitfalls which sometimes catch out the uninitiated. It also covers such things as pre-riding exercise; suitable clothing so as to avoid painful rubs and sores; coping with

and avoiding stiffness; and finding suitable tack which is comfortable for you.

The second and third chapters discuss how your body is affected by riding, and the muscles that are most obviously used; also how to breathe correctly, and what other activities can complement riding and riding fitness. Exercises suitable for the rider, and programmes to build up fitness are included, as well as practical advice on keeping fit if you are not an exercise fanatic.

The second part of the book is geared to the horse and how to get it fit and generally look after it. Knowing that many readers are unlikely to be able to keep their horses stabled full time, I have included some advice on improving the fitness of the grass-kept horse as well as the partially stabled horse. Guidance is given on how to monitor fitness, and train for the specific sports for which you are aiming; also how to cope in hot and humid weather conditions, both of which can have an adverse effect on performance regardless of how fit the horse is at the time.

The last two chapters deal more with specific fitness for the main activities, and how to combine work with pleasure. Also, useful hints on how to cope with minor ailments; going on outings; and the various other useful equine fitness methods available. Riding as a therapy, a concept now becoming more widely recognised and increasingly popular, is covered, as well as tips on how to get involved with the many different aspects of riding.

All in all riding is for enjoyment, and knowing how to prepare yourself and your horse is what it is all about. This book is designed to help you to achieve your aims with the minimum of stress, with useful advice and guidance on getting you and your horse fit for fun.

1  THE NOVICE RIDER

Riding is one of those pastimes which once experienced (probably on a safe, good horse) is never forgotten. Being wholly in charge of another creature – controlling and steering it, influencing how it moves and to where – is quite an exhilarating sensation in itself, not to mention the tremendous feeling of power and motion which can only be experienced when actually on top of a horse. Only then does one truly realise the qualities and skill required from both horse and rider, in the rider's case particularly balance so as to remain in control *as well as* to convey to the horse the various aids requisite for steering or change of pace.

However, it does not take long to feel tired on a horse, certainly for the beginner, as riding is one of the very few occupations where almost every muscle in the body is brought into play as the horse moves. If you are not to tense up against this, it is essential that you learn to relax as much as possible as you ride; and balance becomes vital as you attempt more. Even the horse walking is strenuous for a rider to start with.

● *A range of riding clothes (from left to right): jodhpurs and jodhpur boots; full-length chaps and jodhpur boots; stretch cord breeches and hunting boots; cord breeches with half-length chaps and jodhpur boots; standard breeches with hunting boots*

For those who have never ridden before it is worth taking a few precautions to prevent unnecessary stiffness, and to prepare yourself so that you can progress as quickly as possible – although an active person will probably be fairly fit anyway. If you live in a house with stairs, these provide a wonderful way of using the thigh and calf muscles, which take most of the weight when riding; also, the hips, knees and ankle joints need to be supple, and flexion of these is one of the most important points to bear in mind when riding. Walking up and down stairs a few times extra a day will help to loosen the joints and tone up muscles.

Some people find it difficult to relax properly when taking exercise – they also tend to hold their breath, which of course accentuates the problem. Be sure that you are conscious of breathing evenly, and remember to do so when you ride the horse. Some people when they attempt more quite obviously hold their breath, and it is impossible to relax muscles in this state.

Suitable Clothing

Before attempting to ride make sure you have the sort of clothes which will give you adequate protection. A skullcap is essential and must be securely fastened when you are on the horse. Proper riding jodhpurs or breeches are, of course, best since they are designed to protect the knees with extra padding, but failing these wear stout jeans with tights or leggings underneath. The knees, calves and seatbones are most susceptible to rubs and sores due to the unaccustomed friction and pressure on these vulnerable spots, so an extra padding in

● *This rider is sitting correctly in the saddle, and is wearing breeches and boots which give ideal protection. The heel should always be lower than the toe, with the ball of the foot resting on the stirrup. Gloves should always be worn when riding to prevent soreness*

● *Unsuitable footwear for riding: there is no heel to prevent the foot slipping through the stirrup. Although jeans might be acceptable at first, they will not be comfortable once the rider progresses to more energetic paces*

these areas is beneficial. As you become more proficient you will be better able to control your leg movements and will have a more secure seat in the saddle; you will then be subject to less friction in sensitive areas, and so it will be less of a problem as time goes on.

However, your skin is likely to be soft anyway, so be careful not to do too much too soon. Even to this day I still get sore riding some horses, and certain saddles may also catch you in a particular spot. Toughening up the skin with surgical spirit (rubbing alcohol) – though never apply it on broken skin – you will go through the roof! – and then a dusting with talcum powder will help.

Riding boots can be of the long hunting-boot type, or short 'jodhpur' boots: both are excellent, and the former are popular in rubber. The important feature is that the boot has a heel to prevent your foot sliding right through the stirrup, and if you have not got proper boots do ensure that you have a walking-type shoe which has a good heel. This really is vital as terrible accidents have occurred because people have not bothered about this one really crucial point of safety. Thick socks will protect the heel and ankles. Half-leg chaps or full chaps are a popular protection for the legs, although you are unlikely to find these very comfortable until you have mastered the art of sitting on a horse first, as they are a little bulky. Gloves complete the necessary kit.

If you are going for your first lesson to a riding school, a hat of the right size is often provided, and maybe a friend can loan you suitable boots: these two items are vital for safety and comfort, even if you get the rest later on – once you have definitely decided that riding is for you!

Knowing Your Own State of Fitness

To be able to improve your own state of fitness you will need to know exactly *how* fit you are before you start. The best way to judge this is by knowing your *resting* pulse rate and your breathing rate (how many beats/breaths per minute) and by assessing how easy it is for you to manage mild exercise. It is amazing how this can vary from person to person. Everyone has a slightly different metabolic rate, but the important thing to monitor is how quickly pulse and breathing return to normal after exercise. In theory, the lower the pulse rate the fitter the person, as the heart is not having to work so hard when the pulse rate is slower. Certainly my own pulse rate slowed down once I had made a conscious effort to get fit and was training seriously for the Olympics. Thus at the age of nineteen to twenty my resting pulse was around the seventy mark, but as I got fitter and by the time we left when I could run five miles slowly, do eight hundred backward skips and swim one-and-a-half lengths underwater quite easily, my pulse rate had slowed to fifty-six. I have managed to maintain it at around sixty ever since by remaining fairly active and by keeping up my own version of a maintenance programme.

When you start monitoring your own fitness, watch the rise in pulse rate. This may double, or even rise to nearly three times your normal rate after very strenuous exercise, but the fitter you become the quicker it should return to normal. With medium work it may rise to somewhere round the hundred-and-twenty mark, but when you are reasonably fit it should have dropped back twenty to thirty beats after fifteen to thirty seconds or so, and another thirty beats after a minute.

It is important that you build up distance and then speed slowly so that you do not overstress yourself. The more you do in controlled 'workouts' the easier it will become for your breathing to return to normal. This will then allow the pulse rate to reach normal levels more speedily.

Building Up Stamina

To ride you need to be moderately fit if you are going to get the best out of it, although riding itself is one of the best ways of solving the problem, along with brisk walks or jogs as often as possible – being sure to breathe in and out correctly as you go! Increase the distance gradually, and if you run keep it steady – and *walk* down the hills, as running puts an enormous strain on the knees. It is all right to run uphill, however, if you have built yourself up gradually to do this.

To build up stamina, the importance of starting slowly and building up gradually cannot be over-emphasised – never push yourself too much, but keep trying to increase a little each day. Have an objective to work to: keep it realistic, but always progressive.

There are two ways of working progressively: by *intensifying* the effort, such as running faster over a set distance; and by *increasing the duration*, that is, by doing the same work for longer. The latter is perhaps the best for riders, as you are more likely to ride for longer periods but not necessarily at a faster pace, rather than more intensively – unless you are preparing to race, which requires a rather different approach and one beyond the scope of this book.

Weight and Diet

Inevitably your weight plays quite a significant role in how easy it is to get yourself fit for riding. A neat figure not only looks good on a horse, it is also able to sit in a better position with the muscles able to work more effectively; too much fat makes it difficult for the rider to adopt a good riding position. No one who is overweight can really achieve proper fitness, so if you are on the heavy side it is certainly worth considering how to lose some of those inches. Riding, with its inherent exercise value, will help you to do this anyway, but further exercise will also help you to feel and to look better; although take care to undertake any exercise programme gradually, co-ordinating it with a sensible high energy but low fat diet.

Many diets are difficult to maintain, but undoubtedly there is something that will suit you. I am not, personally, a great believer in too much dieting – I find that by eating a little less, cutting down on in-between snacks, and cutting out a few cups of coffee, I get down to my ideal weight quite easily. However, this is easier for some than for others, and everyone has to find out what works best for him. The following suggested activities and exercises should help.

Fitness Exercise and Activities

Cycling

This is traditionally an excellent form of exercise for the rider, as it works all the relevant muscles. Even better without a seat, one is told, although I cannot think of anything more lethal than inadvertently sitting back on the stump that should hold the seat! However, by riding the bike with your bottom *off* the seat you definitely have to use your thigh and calf muscles more, which helps to build them up, and their strength is important for riding effectively. It also helps to supple hip, knee and ankle joints, as well as being strenuous enough to burn up lots of calories if you keep at it! Breathe in and out regularly. Cycling is excellent for developing all the required muscles evenly, especially if you build up the distances covered progressively.

● *Cycling: an excellent all-round exercise, which is even more strenuous if you ride off the seat*

Swimming

This is another all-round form of exercise which is particularly valuable for riders. It is also useful if you have pulled a muscle or strained yourself, as no weight is borne by any part of the anatomy. Fast times are not so necessary, but using the different strokes will help to exercise all parts of the body. Swimming breaststroke, crawl, backstroke and butterfly will make sure that arms and legs are brought into action evenly and will help to loosen the shoulders and strengthen the arms, and it will build up your breathing mechanism so vital for all-round fitness.

I used to start with a couple of lengths slowly in crawl and breaststroke and build up on this, and then introduce a length at a time of the other strokes. Build up gradually, remembering to concentrate on breathing correctly in and out; never hold your breath for long periods. I used to swim underwater, too, increasing the distance as my ability to hold my breath improved; however nowadays this is felt to be negative training, as you are starving your body of oxygen when you should be thinking of keeping it more in an aerobic state for this type of fitness. In those days the importance of maintaining normal breathing was rarely mentioned.

● *Swimming helps breathing and all-round fitness. Try to use the different strokes. Correct breathing is particularly important to get the full benefit*

Walking and Jogging

This is one of the traditional ways of increasing fitness. A brisk walk is just as strenuous as a slow jog at the same pace, but again it is the gradual increase in either pace or distance which will help to make you fitter. There are all sorts of combinations of walking, running and doing a bit of both which you can adapt to suit yourself. Make sure you have comfortable shoes – there are so many to choose from nowadays, but those with a bit of cushioning will help protect against jarring. Loose-fitting, light clothing is also more comfortable and allows greater freedom.

For those who are very unfit, start with a brisk walk for a quarter to half an hour and build up gradually. A slow walk averages about 2 to 2½ miles per hour; 3 miles per hour is considered a moderate pace, and 4 miles per hour is fast. Few people can walk faster than 5 miles per hour. It is quite fun to measure out a couple of miles or so and see how quickly you can walk or jog this; then you can continue to build up either the distance or the speed.

● *Jogging is something that everyone can do. Make sure you have comfortable shoes, and increase your speed and distances gradually*

● *The author, skipping with a lunge rein in the absence of a real rope! Skipping is particularly useful in helping with correct breathing, and improving balance and fitness*

As a Girl Guide I used to go for miles at 'Scouts' pace (twenty paces walking, twenty paces running) and this principle can be adapted to suit different people – for example forty paces running, twenty paces walking. Concentrated walking or jogging is best undertaken about three times a week, but if you are also trying to lose a bit of weight then the more you do the better, such as four or five times weekly.

Some people may prefer to go jogging straightaway: again, start slowly and build up the distance first, rather than trying to increase the speed too soon. Always feel that you are exercising yourself without strain. If it feels exhausting, ease off and build up more slowly, or walk for a minute in between jogging sessions – these may be from one to three minutes duration, or whatever feels comfortable. Experiment with yourself, but try to keep it sensible yet progressive. It can be fun doing it with a friend – a bit of talking will prevent it from getting too serious, as well as ensuring you breathe well.

Skipping

This can be a strenuous form of exercise, depending how much you decide to do. It can be done forwards or backwards, but the latter is better for deportment and more beneficial for the rider. And because you have to breathe properly to be able to continue skipping, this will also help towards overall riding fitness. Remember to start slowly and to maintain a rhythm, and work up from approximately fifty skips to about a thousand if you are feeling energetic. The continuous movement required, and the fact that breathing correctly is so important whilst doing this, makes this form of exercise particularly similar to riding a horse.

Other Exercise

Apart from the above, most sports help to improve or maintain fitness, although some, if done seriously, can develop more muscle on one side than another – for example tennis and squash. In moderation these can only be beneficial to fitness, but it is worth bearing in mind that to engage in such sports seriously may not be helpful to your riding, where *even* suppleness is important.

Dancing and Aerobics: These are very good forms of exercise. The more energetic dancing will help with overall fitness and stamina.

Gyms and Fitness Centres: Using any of the apparatus to be found in gyms and fitness centres will help to tone up muscles and increase general fitness – but again, beware of overdoing any one part of the body. Any exercises that supple and stretch muscles and joints will be beneficial, so long as they do not excessively overdevelop and harden those muscles.

Press-ups: These can be very useful if you ride strong horses; they are quite tiring, but they certainly helped me become strong enough to control my Badminton winner Warrior who was the hardest-pulling horse I had ever ridden. They should not really be necessary for the beginner or part-time rider, but if you do have problems with a strong horse or if your arm muscles are weak, they will help. However, before attempting press-ups other specific exercises should be done to strengthen the arms first.

There are numerous other exercises that can be used for general all-round fitness, but these are up to the individual, along with treadmills, cycling and rowing machines. There is no need to overdo any of these – but again, if they improve your overall fitness they will be of help. At the end of the day the horse is doing at least fifty per cent of the work; you have only to concentrate on influencing how it goes and what it does!

● *Press-ups are especially useful for strengthening the arm muscles, and are invaluable if you ride a very strong horse. This is particularly strenuous – even one or two are hard work to start with – so make sure you start slowly*

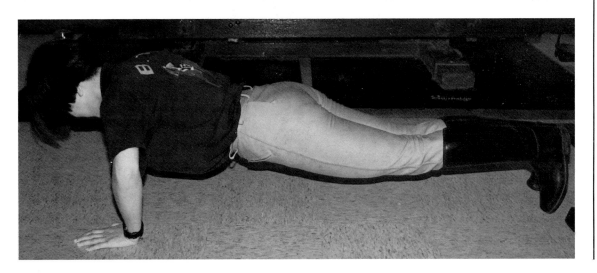

Learning to Ride

Mounting

Getting on and off your horse is obviously one of the primary aspects of learning to ride, and certainly mounting may require a fair bit of stretching and pulling as well as spring. There are three recognised ways of getting on a horse: the first involves mounting from the ground; the second is when a helper gives you a 'leg-up' into the saddle; and the third is by using a mounting block, a raised platform from which it is easier to place your foot in the stirrup and step onto the horse. In all cases *both* stirrup irons should be down, ready for mounting.

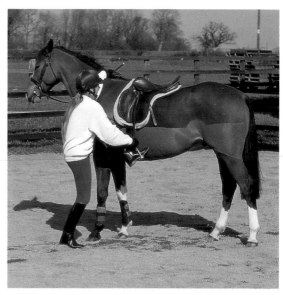

The first method, mounting from the ground, is quite easy so long as your horse is not too high. The following procedure is adopted:

1 Stand on the left side (the nearside) of the horse; take up the reins – which should already be in place on the wither ready for riding – in your left hand, and face towards the horse's rear end.

2 With the right hand, take hold of the right-hand side of the stirrup and turn it towards you: this ensures that the leather will lie flat against your leg once you have settled in the saddle. You can assess how long/short the leather should be for your length of leg like this: put your knuckles against the stirrup bar on the saddle, and the (attached) leather should be as long as the underside of your arm, with the stirrup iron fitted snug up into your armpit.

3 Raise your left leg and put your foot into the stirrup; place your right arm on top of the saddle, swivel your body towards the horse and flex your knees ready to push upwards taking your weight onto the stirrup iron. The left hand with the reins can hold ideally a neckstrap, or a bit of mane, or the pommel of the saddle for security.

● *It is most important that the horse stands still for what is probably the hardest aspect of riding – getting on! Once you've mastered this, the rest should be plain sailing! Remember not to hit the horse's quarters as you take your leg over the back of the saddle*

4 Keep your weight forwards and raise your right leg high enough to go over the saddle; gently ease yourself down into the saddle, and with your right foot find the other stirrup iron.

5 Adjust your weight centrally in the saddle, making sure that your stirrups are level, and that the leathers are adjusted to the right length for your length of leg. Check your girths: you should not be able to run your fingers (flat) between the girth and the horse's belly. As a beginner your helper should do this for you; he/she will stand in front to check that your irons are even.

6 Take up the reins in both hands, and you are ready to go!

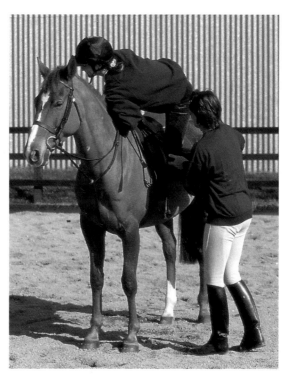

● *For a leg-up to be really successful you should stand close to the horse, and rider and helper must both agree on a course of action*

● *To alter the stirrup length you must first move your leg away from the saddle, and then adjust the leather up or down. Ease the buckle back to the stirrup bar, leaving the end of the leather behind your leg*

● *Remember to move your leg forward quietly before lifting the saddle flap to tighten the girth*

The second method is to have a leg-up, which requires co-ordination between you and your helper, and a bit of spring from you!

1 Stand facing the saddle on the nearside of the horse with the reins in your left hand; your helper should stand behind you.

2 Lift your left foot and bend it at the knee, bracing your muscles ready for lifting; have both hands on the saddle, one on the pommel with the reins and the other on the seat. (Never pull on the cantle as this will twist the tree of the saddle)

3 Your helper should then take hold of your left leg, placing one hand just below the knee and the other above the ankle.

4 Between you, arrange a sequence of indications for lifting: for example, you might say – one, two, three, lift! – at which point you spring lightly upwards, swinging your right leg up and over the saddle as you reach that height.

5 Ease down gently as you move your hands to take up the reins. Find your stirrups and straighten yourself in the saddle ready to move off.

The third method requires a calm, obedient horse willing to stand still and close to your mounting block; really he needs to have been taught to stand like this. If not, it would be sensible to have someone to keep him still and close until you have mastered how to mount this way.

1 Stand the horse with his nearside close up to your mounting block; stand on the block, taking the reins in the left hand.
2 Bend forwards and place your left foot into the stirrup iron, then swing your right leg over the saddle, balancing if necessary with your right hand on the front arch of the saddle.
3 Lower yourself into the saddle, put your feet into the stirrup irons, adjust your weight centrally and take up the reins.

● *Both feet must be out of the stirrups before swinging your leg over and descending slowly to the ground. Talk to your horse quietly before making any sudden movements. Again, make sure you lift your leg high enough to avoid the horse's quarters*

In all cases it is important that your feet are in the irons correctly, and once you have sorted yourself out, to check that your girths are tight enough before moving off.

Dismounting

First bring the horse to a halt: be sure that he is obedient and does not move off. Keep hold of the reins, and take both feet out of the stirrups. Swing your weight forwards and bring your right leg up and over his back – then slide down onto the ground on the nearside, remembering to bend your knees on landing. Run your irons up the leathers on both sides. Take the reins over the horse's head ready to lead him back to the stable or paddock.

It is most important to keep your weight forwards and to bend your knees when landing off the horse so that you do not lose your balance. Mounting and dismounting require suppleness and co-ordination and it will take a few practices before you find this part easy.

1

Position in the Saddle

Once mounted, the rider must understand the importance of sitting straight on the horse at all times. This is perhaps the single most vital aspect of riding, because without straightness in the saddle you can never be truly effective – not only does it influence all your own efforts, but failure to sit straight will soon seriously inhibit what the horse is able to do underneath you. The horse's centre of gravity is just behind the withers, and straightness above this, on a well fitting saddle, is the first step.

Once you have arranged yourself centrally in the saddle we will go through the positioning of the body as it should be, starting at the top.

● *In this picture the author is tending to tip forwards a little with her hands low on the neck and insufficient weight in the stirrup to give an effective, firm lower leg position*

● *This rider is doing the opposite: leaning back on the horse and tightening her arms into a straight line, giving a stiff, unnatural appearance. Her leg position, however, is fairly good*

1 The head should be held upright and straight, looking ahead at all times. If the head is poked forward it will seriously affect the balance of the rider and ultimately the horse – quite apart from the fact that it looks bad in the first place.

2 The shoulders should be square and relaxed downwards. Beginners may well tense upwards here, and it is most important that this does not happen. Encourage correct breathing, and a lowering of the shoulders from the start: suggest to the rider that he rolls the shoulders upwards and backwards as he relaxes down into the saddle, so that he at least starts in the correct position.

3 The arms should fall naturally to the elbows, which should be level, and then there should be a natural straight line from the bend in the elbow through the wrist to the hand. This should be maintained through all riding if the hands are held correctly just above the withers. On a well-balanced, collected horse the hands will be held higher than on one which is on its forehand.

4 The hands are to a certain extent, and certainly in the early stages of riding, the rider's main means of steering and control; to encourage a favourable reaction from the horse they must be soft and sensitive to its responses at all times. They should be held upright with the palms facing inwards, and the fingers – which must *always* be flexible – lightly holding the reins. With single reins, the rider normally holds each rein so that it rests between the third and fourth fingers, then over the palm and between the thumb and first finger.

With double reins it is the same idea, but with the bridoon (snaffle) rein passing on the outside of the little finger whilst the curb rein passes between the little and third fingers. Alternatively the reins can be crossed so that the curb rein is on the outside.

The thumb should always rest on top, with the wrists allowed to curl naturally slightly inwards and never held stiffly. It is the hands at the end of the reins which ultimately govern how the horse goes, and it cannot be over-emphasised how important it is for the rider to maintain soft and relaxed hands when riding.

5 The body should be upright with a straight, but *never* hollow back – it should be erect, but never stiff and must always respond with suppleness to the movement of the horse.

6 The seat is the basis for effective riding and must be secure and supple. If the back is straight and not hollow the rider is generally sitting correctly on the seatbones. He should be seated centrally in the lowest part of the saddle, with his weight evenly distributed; any tendency to hollow the back will immediately shift him forwards onto his 'fork' (pubic bone). Riders should therefore think of 'tucking their backsides underneath', which will restore them to the correct position.

7 The legs should be allowed to hang downwards in a natural way, with a bend at the knee and a light contact with the horse's sides at all times. They should be level, with the weight of the body divided equally between the feet resting in the stirrups: it is most important to maintain an even weight in both stirrups, and not to let one leg move forwards and back more than the other except when it is necessary to correct or influence the horse's way of going. The ankles should be flexible, with the weight generally going down into these; they act as shock absorbers, and it is important always to think of 'weight into heel' so that a firm leg position is established. The seat and leg positions are vital to good riding: a close, supple and secure seat and a correct, firm leg position are the basis for success.

8 The joints of the body must remain flexible and supple at all times if your riding is to achieve maximum effect. The hip and ankle joints perhaps need to be the most flexible, especially when the stirrup leathers are shortened for galloping and jumping – once this happens, the angles of the body become much more acute and bring all joints much more into play; moreover it may take a little time to loosen and stretch muscles and joints sufficiently to be able to do this without discomfort. Riding with short leathers in the jumping position for gradually lengthening periods will help to increase fitness for this. Do not attempt too much too soon, particularly if you feel your joints or muscles aching, but wait until you can canter short comfortably for five to ten minutes before jumping.

Your position in the saddle must feel and look straight and balanced from the front, side and rear. It is a good idea to stand up in the stirrups to ensure that your weight is evenly distributed, and that you have a feel of equal weight in both stirrups. The beginner will find it easier to lean very slightly forwards when the horse moves, until he is used to the feeling of movement.

In walk the hands should travel forwards and backwards in rhythm to the horse's movement; they should not remain rigid. Because the walk is a four-time movement, each hoof falling individually in sequence, the horse needs reasonable freedom to be able to move happily. The rider's torso must absorb this movement, with a loose and supple lower back which must nonetheless remain erect from the waist.

In trot the horse moves in two-time, each diagonal pair of hooves together in turn. The rider will need to keep his balance forwards and should rise out of the saddle pushing the weight down into the heel on one diagonal, then sink down into the saddle as the horse moves onto the other diagonal. The pelvis will go forward a little in the upward movement and will then straighten before returning back to the saddle. It is most important not to lose balance and bang down on to the saddle at this point, which can happen if the rider's weight gets too far back. The hands should remain quiet and still just above the withers.

In sitting trot the rider keeps his seat in the saddle and allows his back, seat, thighs, knees and ankles to absorb the movement. Some horses have an easier trot to sit to than others, but relaxation into the movement of the horse is the secret. Softness in the thighs will ensure you do not get thrown back up out of the saddle, which is a common fault. All movement should be absorbed through the supple back – on no account should the rider bump on the horse's back, he must keep his seat firmly in the saddle.

In canter the horse's hooves fall as three beats – for example near-hind, off-hind and near-fore together, then off-fore – and its body alters from a forward-and-down position to a rebalancing upward one as it pre-pares for the next stride. The rider's body must move with the horse as it alters its position in this slightly forward and back motion; however, he should do this through his seat and lower back, rather than by moving the shoulders or upper back. The hands should move slightly to follow the movement of each stride, and the rider must be sure that as the horse stretches forwards his hands go forwards too, rather than restricting the movement by holding back; this is a remarkably common fault.

When turning or circling in canter, the rider's inside leg should be in a slightly forward position on the girth, with the outside one a little further back controlling the hind quarters. Take care not to lean inwards, but remain centrally in the saddle with the weight distributed equally in the stirrup irons.

At all times and in all paces *concentrate on remaining relaxed*. If you feel yourself tensing up, slow down, and if necessary start again and build up confidence gradually.

Remember to breathe normally – not doing so is a very common problem which will readily afflict a rider when he is concentrating hard on getting things right! Please remember that without oxygen the body will not function anyway, so you will never get it right if you do not give yourself the chance! Some people find it helps to count, some sing, some just talk until they relax enough to breathe normally. Even experienced riders sometimes find this difficult, so it is important to try and get it right at the beginning.

At the end of each lesson try to spend a short time thinking of relaxation, with your mind concentrating on the most important factors:

1 Straightness in the saddle
2 Developing a deep seat in the saddle with your weight going down the leg into the heel
3 Soft sensitive hands
4 Supple back with an erect but not stiff body
5 Head looking up and ahead
6 Breathing normally

THE WALK (Four-beat movement)

1: Off hind

2: Off fore

3: Near hind

4: Near fore

THE TROT (Two-beat movement)

1: Left diagonal (near hind and off fore)

2: Right diagonal (off hind and near fore)

THE CANTER (Three-beat movement)

1: Near hind

2: Off hind and near fore

3: Off fore (leading)

Controlling the Horse

Once mounted, the sensation of movement comes as quite a surprise to many; in particular, the four-beat sequence of the horse's walk causes a slight rocking movement forwards and backwards. To ask the horse to move forwards, a strong squeeze or slight vibration with the heels and lower leg should be all that is required. If this is insufficient to indicate 'move' to the horse, try a stronger 'kick' with the heels. Some horses are more sensitive than others, so when assessing a horse's reactions always start by being too gentle rather than too strong, otherwise you may move rather more quickly than you intended! The rider should control the degree of forward momentum by the reins with a give-and-take motion rather than a continuous pull; keep the hands low.

Once the horse is moving, try to relax your muscles so that they are effective for the next command. It is easy to overdo everything when you are starting off and a particular problem is to remain tense and hold the breath: relax and breathe normally while you practise moving forwards and stopping. All beginners should have an instructor walking with them, who should be ready to offer guidance but without preventing the rider from finding out how to do things for himself. The horse should be kept on a lunge line until the rider is proficient at stopping and starting.

Considerable effort may be required, especially as horses which are quiet enough for beginners to use are not generally very responsive to the leg – they often react more promptly to the voice, with a 'walk on' or 'whoa'. The beginner will also find that he needs to be co-ordinated to a surprising degree when using the reins and the legs at the same time, especially when one of these has to be a little stronger than the other.

When asking the horse to change from one pace to another it is most important that the rider keeps his weight forwards so that his balance is not upset as the horse increases or decreases its speed. If in doubt lean forwards, re-establish your position, then start again.

Controlling Direction

To indicate to the horse that you wish to go in a different direction, take a stronger feel on the rein on the side you wish to turn towards. You should then squeeze with your outside leg (opposite – that is, right rein, left leg, for example), as the legs control the quarters of the horse – thus you will be using the sequence 'inside hand with outside leg'. The beginner will probably only be able to cope with the hand to start with, but the principle should be learnt from the beginning: the earlier you learn the correct procedure the better, and then the sooner you will become a proficient rider.

Never do too much too soon: thus concentrate on mastering the essentials at walk before going on to trot. And you must be able to stop, start and change direction confidently before you try on your own.

You will soon feel which muscles are having to work hard and which are not; and there is no general rule as to which will be most generally affected, as everyone is different. The secret is to use the aids, whether from the hand, seat or leg, to get a reaction, and once this is achieved to reduce the pressure – this acts as a 'reward' for the horse who has responded to your wishes.

When steering the horse, many beginners make the mistake of crossing the hand over the neck, and in effect this creates as much pull on the other side of the horse's mouth – it creates a 'block'; the hands must therefore stay on each side of the neck just above the withers, and not cross over. If necessary shorten the reins or take the hand out a little, especially when schooling young horses, to give a better indication of direction.

Straightness is most important, so an even feel on the reins is essential; besides, it will be much easier to get a reaction to turn if the horse has been going straight in the first place. Unfortunately not every horse goes equally well in both directions; like us they tend to be somewhat one-sided, and this is partly because we tend to do everything with them from one side. We normally lead, mount, dismount and so on, all from the nearside so the majority of horses tend to become rather stiff on the left.

CONTROLLING DIRECTION

stronger feel on inside rein asks for flexion

outside shoulder forward, parallel with horse's shoulders

inside leg on the girth

outside leg behind the girth

horse leans on left rein

left hand against neck to stop shoulder falling out

right rein guides the forehand to the right

left leg on the girth asking for forward movement

right leg behind the girth

hindquarters swinging out to right

LEFT: **Turning the horse**

Take a stronger feel on the rein which is on the side you wish to turn towards. The inside leg should be on the girth (see *Applying the leg aids* below); think of bending the horse around this leg. The outside leg, which is applied behind the girth, controls the horse's hindquarters, stopping them from falling out as he turns. Your outside shoulder should come forward a little to stay parallel with the horse's shoulders.

As you become more experienced you will learn to use the seat aids in addition, pushing forward onto the inside seatbone and putting more weight on the inside stirrup.

CENTRE AND RIGHT: **Straightness**

Most horses are born with a stiffness on one side,

in the same way that we are either right or left-handed. Few horses will move in a straight line; the hindquarters swing out, usually to the right, and they lean on the left shoulder and consequently the left rein. To make the best use of the energy created in the hindquarters, the horse must be kept straight so that the energy is not lost through the shoulders.

To correct the crookedness the rider guides the forehand to the right, using the right rein, until the forehand is on the same tracks as the hindquarters. The left hand is against the neck to stop the left shoulder falling out. The right leg, applied behind the girth, pushes the right hindleg inside while the left leg remains on the girth and asks for forward movement.

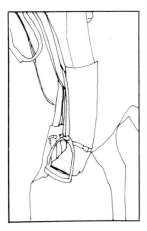

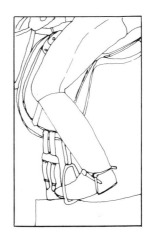

Applying the leg aids

LEFT: The inside leg is applied on the girth by closing the lower leg and ankle against the horse's side. As you do this don't twist your foot or the back of your heel will dig into his side. The inside leg creates impulsion and the horse should bend around that leg when you are turning.

RIGHT: The outside leg is applied behind the girth to stop the hindquarters from falling out on a turn

A small dressage arena 20m (66ft) by 40m (132ft), correctly marked out.
An international size dressage arena measures 20m (66ft) by 60m

Simple Exercises to Help Control

Once the rider is confident enough to be let off the lunge, he must learn to do turns and circles on his own. First at walk, practise turning to the right and then the left and periodically come back to a halt; all the time remember to apply the leg when you need it, to turn, stop or move forwards. Acquire that vital element of 'feel': you must be able to assess each horse you sit on, and know how much leg or hand will be required; to discover whether you are on a sensitive or an idle horse, one that is quick or slow, and be able to react to it accordingly. As with people, to get the best out of your horse you need to 'sus them out' and 'tune into their wavelength' if you are to build up a good working relationship. Horses are not machines, but living creatures with feelings and fears like ourselves, who can often seem unpredictable if you have not made the effort to try to understand how they think.

Another exercise is to place poles at random on the ground: the rider then walks his horse over the middle of each pole, and effectively steers by using both hands and legs to indicate direction.

A school with dressage markers encourages the rider to move to different markers and halt. Watch to see if he is improving his leg aids, and whether the hands are becoming more sensitive. When confident, these exercises can be done in trot.

A nervous rider may need to be put back on the lunge for a couple of trotting sessions, especially if it is a free-going horse.

The above exercises help to develop independence and confidence; they also teach the rider where the dressage markers are, an awareness which may come in useful later. Work over poles also builds confidence and is an ideal preparation for jumping. If the rider learns to approach poles in the centre, he will soon find that jumping comes quite easily. Circles are another excellent exercise, since the beginner often has great difficulty in making a circle look anything like round! Co-ordination between hand and leg is essential, and knowing how much to use of each requires a great deal of practice. Start with large circles, then gradually reduce their size until you can work on a few smaller ones. To start with, the rider will find it difficult to keep his balance on the smaller ones, and must concentrate on keeping his weight evenly in both stirrups and staying straight in the saddle without collapsing the inside hip.

To help balance and co-ordination, the rider might practise keeping his seat out of the saddle for three strides: thus, rise for three, then stay out of the saddle for three, then rise again for three strides, and so on. Another version is to sit for a few strides, then rise, then sit again. However, be careful not to do too much sitting trot in the early stages, at least until you are riding confidently and in a good basic position; it is very easy to slide to the back of the saddle so that your legs come too far forwards. You must relax your back and thighs sufficiently so that you do *not* bump in the saddle.

The above exercises can be done off the lunge without too much cause for anxiety; however, for the more specific exercises it is best for the horse to be on the lunge so that the rider can concentrate on what he is doing rather than worrying about the horse. From a safety point of view this is sensible, and the rider will gain maximum benefit from the exercises. (See Chapter 2 for a wide range of exercises designed to help those wanting to improve their position and their effectiveness in the saddle.)

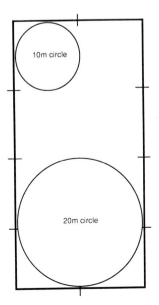

10m circle

20m circle

Comfortable Tack

Once you have mastered the basics of riding you may want to take it up more seriously, and if you already have a horse then you will probably be feeling quite ambitious. If so, the tack you use is important. To ride comfortably you must have a saddle that is the right size for you and your horse and one in which you feel secure, that does not force you into an unnatural position but assists you to ride effectively.

The Saddle

Saddles come in three main designs: dressage, general purpose and jumping:

The dressage saddle is designed so that the rider is encouraged to ride with a longer leg. The saddle flap is cut fairly straight, and generally it has a fairly deep seat which effectively keeps the rider in one position. This may be fine for many, but it can sometimes have the effect of pushing the rider too far

forwards, onto his 'fork' thus encouraging a hollow back, rather than helping him to stay upright and sit more on the seatbones. However, there are many excellent dressage saddles on the market and the rider should try out any saddle well – the saddler should see it on the horse and when he is mounted to be quite sure it is a good fit.

Remember that all saddles will need checking periodically in case they need restuffing or restitching.

The general purpose saddle is designed for those who want to do a bit of everything, from dressage to jumping to hacking and hunting, and is probably the saddle of choice to start with. The saddle is more forward-cut so the rider can shorten the stirrups a little more, and allows for a more versatile style of riding.

The jumping saddle has an even more forward-cut panel to allow for the much shorter leg position customary for galloping and jumping, and thus makes it easier for the rider to shift his seat further back in the saddle as the angle from the shoulders, hips to heel is increased.

● *The three most common saddles (from left to right): general purpose; dressage; jumping*

Most modern saddles have knee padding to prevent chafing in this vulnerable area. Some saddles have a lot of panel padding, but this tends to push you rather too far away from the horse even when the saddle has been worked in. Avoid saddles that force you away from the horse: the best are those that keep you as close as possible. The saddle must also be a good fit on the horse, with a clear channel between the panels on either side of the spine. It must not press down too low over the withers and should rest evenly over the back. The tree must be wide enough for the horse too: there are three basic widths – narrow, medium and wide. If the tree is too narrow it will pinch the horse on either side of the withers; too wide, and it will press down on the withers – both can adversely affect the animal's way of going.

Most modern saddles have a spring tree which has a little more 'give' and is much more comfortable for the rider. However, many have a deep seat and this does concentrate the weight in one area on the horse's back. I prefer the flatter type of seat which enables the rider to adopt a position comfortable for him, and which allows the seat to move forwards or back with ease. Everyone, however, has a different preference!

Saddle Accessories

Check that the **girths** are comfortable, the right length for the horse and that they fit easily onto the girth straps. Many of the newer saddles have extra-wide girth straps which then do not fit the girths! Beware of the dressage saddle with the long girth straps which require a special short girth; the idea is to prevent the bulkiness of the

● *The jumping saddle is the most forward cut of the three, and enables the rider to accentuate the hip-knee-ankle angles necessary for a secure jumping position*

● *The dressage saddle is much more straight cut, encouraging the rider to have the longer leg position essential for dressage. It also encourages a deeper seat*

● *The general purpose saddle enables the rider to both shorten sufficiently for the jumping position and to lengthen the leg position for flatwork*

girth buckles lying under your leg. However good this may seem, they can be extremely difficult to do up once you are mounted, so give it some thought if you are choosing a saddle.

Irons and leathers also come in all shapes, widths, weights and sizes. However, essentially the stirrups must be the right size for your feet: allow at least ¼in between your foot and the inside of the stirrup branch on each side to be sure your foot will fit the stirrup easily. If they are too big there is the risk that the foot will slip right through (though this should not happen if you have a proper heel on your boot).

Some irons are heavy and designed to encourage the rider to push his weight down into them; others are lighter. Always choose steel irons that are the right size and feel comfortable for you. Stirrup leathers should be strong but not bulky; check the stitching regularly, and if it is coming loose get it repaired immediately. Really narrow leathers may not be very strong so choose some that are not too thick but are wide enough to be safe.

Numnahs or pads used under the saddle are popular nowadays and do help to spread the pressure of the mounted rider. Make sure they are attached to the saddle correctly and are not too small for the saddle, otherwise they will push down causing an uneven ridge under the saddle when the rider mounts. Always pull them up well into the front arch of the saddle before tightening the girth so they do not cause pressure across the withers.

The Bridle

The bridle should fit the horse comfortably and be of the correct size for him, with a bit that is neither too wide nor too narrow. The width and style of the reins will affect only the rider: ¾in width is comfortable for most people, but be sure to select the width that really does suit your hands – just that little bit too wide, and your hands will ache. Also, the length of the reins should be relative to the size of your horse: for example, really long ones on a small horse can be dangerous.

There are numerous different designs of

● *Numnahs or pads should always be pulled up into the front arch of the saddle, and should be the right size for the particular saddle*

rein, but choose one that is comfortable. Anything with a slight grip should be helpful, particularly if it rains or if the horse is rather strong. Plaited reins look smart for showing or for dressage; rubber reins are generally used for jumping or hunting. Plain reins are perfectly adequate and probably the most comfortable of all, but you will need good gloves if it rains because they do become slippery. Gloves with the rubber 'pimples' on the palms are cheap and very popular.

For the beginner especially it is a great comfort to have a neckstrap or a martingale which gives added security in case of emergency. I always use a martingale when riding a young horse and there have been many occasions when I have been more than grateful that it was there!

From the horse's point of view it is most important that your tack is well cared for and in good condition. Any stiff leather will

● *This standing martingale enables the rider to use the neckstrap for added security if necessary. It will also prevent the horse putting his head too high and out of the angle of control*

be uncomfortable and may rub, besides which neglected tack risks becoming brittle and therefore much more likely to break under stress. Check stitching on all tack regularly, and *never* leave any stitching that is coming undone 'for another time' – so often this sort of negligence has resulted in a nasty fall.

As with anything, comfort is most important so be sure that your essential saddlery and clothing is comfortable for you. A slight rub anywhere can be excruciatingly painful, and may cause you or the horse to move in an abnormal way. So often it is the apparently insignificant things which lead to incorrect posture or position, and which initiate bad habits.

INTERMEDIATE FITNESS & TRAINING

The next stage of our study is to consider the rider who has ridden quite a bit but is now anxious to improve and become more effective. To be able to do this a little more knowledge is required as to how the horse responds to the rider's wishes – both physically and in his mind – and how the rider should best make his intentions known to the horse. So often a rider is seen asking his mount to perform in such a way that physically it is very difficult for it to co-operate. The result is predictable enough if he really thought about it – but then, it is a well-known human fault that we act before we think!

The Physical Factor

The horse's anatomy and physiology are such that it is quite possible for it to function with a rider on top *as long as* that rider complements its natural way of going, and tones and develops its relevant muscles so that it *can* function more efficiently. To do this without hindering the horse the rider must stay in balance at all times: if he does not do so, the horse will be continually compensating for this shifting of weight by bracing one set of muscles more than others; eventually this could lead to uneven muscle development, which in turn might cause muscle wasting and strain, or lameness in the weakest areas.

The rider should also have a basic understanding of muscle function, as in principle this will affect him in a similar way; it should certainly dictate how he manages his horse in certain situations.

Muscle Function

Muscles function by contracting and relaxing, and are stimulated through the action of nerves. When a muscle receives the stimulus for an action it also receives oxygen and other basic elements necessary to produce sufficient energy for the action required. For increased energetic work the heart beats faster so that in effect the muscles receive the necessary amount of oxygen and nutrients to keep them working efficiently. You should realise that when getting yourself or your horse fit it is most important that your fittening or muscular development is achieved slowly – that is, steadily but not too fast. Muscles will adapt to requirements if they are stimulated regularly in training, so that even if initially they are not very strong, they can be built up gradually to meet the demands of the sort of action required. Thus the jumper will need to jump sufficiently in training to develop the jumping muscle; the dressage horse must regularly perform the movements required in dressage tests particularly when these become more demanding; and the galloping horse will need to gallop, not at particularly excessive speeds but for increasing distances until he is able to do what is required relatively easily. Basically, a steady build-up will enable the horse to tackle his work with ease because progressive training will increase his stamina levels, thanks to the effective ability of the blood supply to feed the muscles accordingly.

There are three main types of muscle which function in different ways according to their situation in the body, and depending upon the effect their action is therefore intended to have.

1 **Skeletal muscle** is designed to enable the skeleton to move. Each muscle consists of millions of elongated cell fibres, joined together at the ends to become the tendons which are attached to the skeletal

THE SKELETON AND MUSCLES
OF THE HORSE

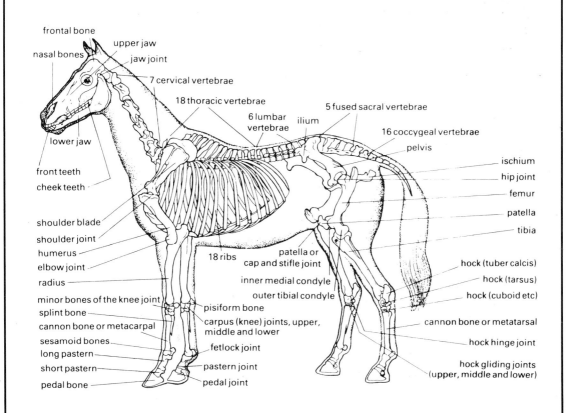

frontal bone
upper jaw
jaw joint
nasal bones
7 cervical vertebrae
18 thoracic vertebrae
6 lumbar vertebrae
ilium
5 fused sacral vertebrae
16 coccygeal vertebrae
pelvis
lower jaw
ischium
hip joint
femur
front teeth
patella
cheek teeth
tibia
shoulder blade
shoulder joint
humerus
elbow joint
18 ribs
patella or cap and stifle joint
hock (tuber calcis)
hock (tarsus)
radius
inner medial condyle
outer tibial condyle
hock (cuboid etc)
minor bones of the knee joint
pisiform bone
splint bone
carpus (knee) joints, upper, middle and lower
cannon bone or metatarsal
cannon bone or metacarpal
sesamoid bones
fetlock joint
hock hinge joint
long pastern
short pastern
pastern joint
hock gliding joints (upper, middle and lower)
pedal bone
pedal joint

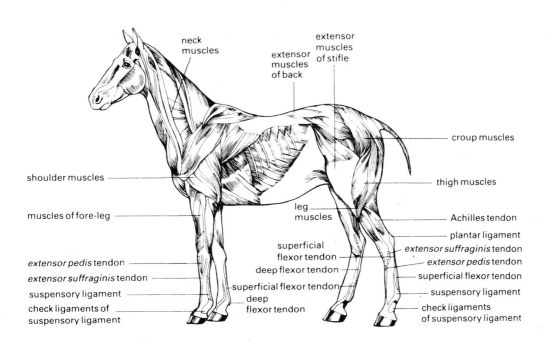

neck muscles
extensor muscles of back
extensor muscles of stifle
croup muscles
shoulder muscles
thigh muscles
muscles of fore-leg
leg muscles
Achilles tendon
plantar ligament
superficial flexor tendon
extensor suffraginis tendon
deep flexor tendon
extensor pedis tendon
extensor pedis tendon
superficial flexor tendon
extensor suffraginis tendon
superficial flexor tendon
suspensory ligament
deep flexor tendon
suspensory ligament
check ligaments of suspensory ligament
check ligaments of suspensory ligament

structure. When the muscles contract, the tendons are caused to pull on the joints/bones, and this enables movement. Muscle cells contain glycogen and enzymes; these are broken down into energy which fuels muscle function.

2 **Cardiac muscle** is found only in the heart, which is basically a hollow pump of muscle. Nervous stimulation and blood pressure are responsible for the pumping action.

3 **Smooth muscle** is generally found in the main organs of the body such as the digestive tract.

The objective of every rider when training should be to train for maximum fitness by teaching the body to utilise oxygen to achieve this. The more oxygen used by the body, the more possible it will be for it to work longer aerobically (with oxygen). Muscle fatigue and tiredness are caused by the using up of the oxygen and glycogen available in the muscle cells – lactic acid, produced in the glycogen-to-energy conversion process, cannot be removed quickly enough by the bloodstream, and builds up in the muscles thus preventing the fibres from working properly. At this stage the body is said to be working anaerobically (without oxygen).

In humans this causes cramp and can be most painful, as probably it does in horses, too; however, they seem to be able to continue for longer than humans in this state. Once the lactic acid is removed in the blood from the muscles they can function normally again. Therefore if either horse or human has worked hard, it is important to be aware that these physiological changes are taking place and allow for a winding-down period to enable them to run their course; the more time spent cooling off and allowing the blood supply to return to its normal functioning at its most effective speed, the less likelihood there will be of stiffness. To stop, and stand or sit still immediately after exertion is not a good idea: wind down gradually.

The Effect of Exercise

Although improving the fitness of the horse and the rider require different techniques, the basics remain the same. Essentially, increased fitness results in the ability of the body to function more efficiently for longer periods. If you understand this principle it is easy to see why, for the serious horseman, the training and fitness of the rider as well as the horse is an important concern. Exercise has the effect of increasing the heart rate as well as the respiration rate, which is why gradually progressive, controlled exercise will increase the ability of heart and lungs to function effectively for longer. The unfit horse or human cannot sustain an effort for very long.

It may not be generally appreciated that the actual heart size is increased as the body uses it more demandingly with a greater amount of exercise. This in turn stimulates the circulation and produces more oxygen in the body; the result of this is that the body can function for longer before getting tired. Such progress can be monitored by noticing the following:

1 A slower resting pulse rate
2 Quicker recovery
3 Lower maximum pulse and respiration rates after set exercise

Some people like to monitor fitness so as to get a clear picture of the progress made. The following chart shows corresponding human and horse pulse and respiration rates. (Further information on the horse's fitness will be found in Chapters 4 and 5.)

COMPARISON CHART OF T, P & R RATES BETWEEN HORSE & HUMAN

	TEMPERATURE	PULSE (Resting)	RESPIRATION
HUMAN	36.6°C (98.4°F)	60–80 beats per minute	16–20 breaths per minute
HORSE	38°C (100–100.5°F)	35–40 beats per minute	8–15 breaths per minute

Various factors such as age, heat, temperament may influence readings

Exercise Routines

For the really determined fitness fanatic there are various special exercise systems which many people have found useful for riding, in particular the Alexander technique and callanetics. Other useful fitness exercises might include voltige (vaulting) performed on the horse; also hand/eye co-ordination exercises and yoga.

Whilst the Alexander technique is not specifically a method of learning to ride, it should nonetheless prove invaluable for those intending to be horsemasters. It is a mind–body technique which aims to promote neuro-muscular development such as assists with balance, poise and general physical well-being. Mentally it develops calmness and rational thinking. It is therefore of benefit to the rider as it will help in improving body control and balance, general co-ordination of the limbs, and calmness.

It is a method whereby the practician is made to be more aware of balance, posture and movement in day-to-day activities. Good posture has been scientifically recognised as essential if the body's natural postural reflexes are to react freely; however, it is also true that the emotional and physical stresses and strains of everyday life soon lead to postural restrictions and lack of balance. To counteract this, and to support our bodies against the ever-present pull of gravity, we must provide the necessary degree of relaxation while retaining the mechanisms of support and balance. With the guidance of the Alexander teacher the rider can loosen, breathe and relax enough so that natural reflexes are encouraged to work again. One particular area where there has been significant improvement is in those suffering back-pain who have adopted the Alexander technique.

Riders should first learn the Alexander principles when not in the saddle, then adopt the procedure for riding once the general level of function has improved. If you are an 'up-tight', nervous type of person it would certainly be worth your while to find out more about this technique.

Callanetics is another very useful and successful technique concerned primarily with firming and toning the deep muscles of the body, particularly those round the buttocks and thighs and that control the body movements. It is particularly successful for those whose figure has become out of shape and flabby, a condition which will prohibit the serious rider from ever looking good or being able to ride really successfully – a course of callanetics could make all the difference as to how well a rider is able to perform on a horse. It also claims to have benefits over and above the usual ones of increasing strength, flexibility and stamina – these include co-ordination and body control, discipline, speed of reactions, physical and mental relaxation, and so on.

Do not become obsessed by weight loss or gain – it is quite usual to put on a few pounds as muscle is transformed and flab disappears. Nor should you be concerned by the changes taking place in your body; for example at certain stages you may well see unexpected lumps of 'flab' appear. In fact this is rather the phenomenon of muscles taking control of certain parts of the body more strongly than others as they tone up – after one or two more sessions you will appreciate a more complete transformation as all your muscles start to work evenly and effectively, and your body becomes more streamlined.

Callanetics comprises one of the few exercise routines where music is discouraged, as it is most important to concentrate on complete mastery of your body movements. With music you tend instinctively to move in time to the beat, instead of making sure you have complete control of your body. The exercises can be done anywhere so long as you are comfortable. Preferably you should have a large mirror so you can check your position and monitor progress. You will also need a 'bar', although a table-top, counter or even a window-sill can be used – essentially something firm to hold on to for some of the exercises, such as those for your legs and hips.

Exercises to promote suppleness are valuable for all riders, as a supple body is so essential for good riding, but they are especially so for the person whose ordinary lifestyle does not involve very much physical action on a day-to-day basis.

EXERCISES TO PROMOTE SUPPLENESS

The following are the classic ones used regularly by jockeys and riders who need to loosen up certain parts of the body. As a rule they should be done slowly with the maximum amount of stretch. Repeat the movements five to ten times, and always remember the importance of a *gradual* build-up: never force your body, but increase progressively to a target which is reasonable *for you*. Always spend the same amount of time on one side as on the other. Generally it is best to start by going through the body systematically. Wear loose-fitting, comfortable clothes – give yourself room, and if at home, make sure you are not in a draught before starting. Some of these exercises can be done just as easily on a horse.

Head and neck exercises These should be done slowly, on or off the horse; if mounted, the horse should be held still. Allow the head to roll forwards, then gradually roll it round in a circular movement stretching the neck muscles as much as possible forwards and back. Repeat two or three times one way before rolling the head in the opposite direction. Do not overdo this – three repeats in each direction would be sufficient.

Arm exercises Again, these can be done on or off the horse. The horse could be walking on the lunge whilst the 'trainer' watches the rider's position and encourages him to maximum effort. Stretching circles, wing stretchers, shoulder shrug are all excellent for loosening and relaxing shoulders, elbows, wrists and arms in general.

Some exercises such as press-ups and push-offs will help to improve strength, and are especially useful for the rider with a really strong horse – I managed to do fifteen press-ups a day before riding Warrior in a three-day event!

Leg exercises The legs should take most of the strain in riding, though in fact this very much depends on how much effort the rider puts into using his legs, and how effective he is.

1 Leg swings These will help to stretch and loosen leg muscles as well as the hip joint. Stand up straight with one arm holding onto a door, ledge or other support and swing the opposite leg as far forwards and as far back as possible. Repeat six to ten times, then do the same exercise with the other leg.

2 Knee bends These are also excellent for strengthening thighs and loosening hip, knee and ankle joints. Stand holding onto a solid bar or support and squat down as low as possible; then stand up again pushing up from the joints, keeping the back as straight as you can throughout. Repeat three to six times, then relax and repeat again.

3 Running on the spot This is another very useful general fitness exercise so long as it is performed correctly: to be effective, the legs must be worked high enough and come off the ground by at least 12in with every step. Start with twenty-five paces and gradually increase as fitness improves. This exercise will help to strengthen all muscles in the legs.

4 Stairs Running up and down stairs is more strenuous than the former exercise and will strengthen back and leg muscles and help with breathing.

5 Ski swings This is a useful general exercise which will actually help with most muscles in the back, arms and legs as well as the main joints in the body. With legs apart, sink down as far as possible, bend the body and rock forwards; swing the arms in a crouched skiing position. Repeat three to six times, then return to the upright starting position.

Additional exercises to try

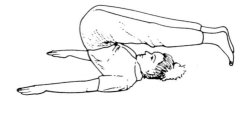

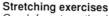

Stretching exercises
Good for strengthening the back, abdominal and inner thigh muscles – and for trimming the waist!

**LEFT AND BELOW LEFT:
Stretching exercises**
These exercises stretch the leg muscles which helps to tone them. They also help to stretch and lengthen the spine which will help you to sit tall and straight in the saddle

BELOW:
An exercise which is very good for strengthening the thigh muscles

You can practise a good upper body jumping position with this exercise. Bend forwards from the hips (use your arm across your lower back to keep it straight) then come up again. Do this several times

Sit-ups strengthen the muscles in the abdomen, back and legs

Raising and lowering the legs is good for strengthening the stomach muscles. Try to hold them in the raised position for a count of ten before slowly lowering them to the floor

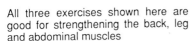
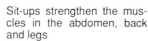

All three exercises shown here are good for strengthening the back, leg and abdominal muscles

These exercises will all help towards building up strength and tone in the muscles which are used in riding, should the rider feel this is necessary. However, riding itself is by far the most useful way of improving basic fitness, and the following routines which can be done on the horse will probably prove effective enough for most people.

For the beginner, the trainer must be careful to assess how much, as a rider, he will be able to do, and should always have safety as the first priority. Always hold on to the horse if the rider is to do exercises on it whilst it stands at halt, and keep him on a lunge rein until he is sufficiently confident and under control.

Exercises When Stationary

Head and neck exercises have already been mentioned (see page 38), and should always be performed with the horse stationary.

● *Care should always be taken to ensure a calm and quiet environment when doing exercises mounted, particularly when doing head and neck exercises. These will help to loosen the neck and shoulder muscles*

1 **Arm swings and stretches** will help to improve confidence and balance as well as suppleness:
   a) Raise to shoulder level, and in sequence bend elbows bringing hands sharply back to chest (three times)
   b) Above head, bring hands back to shoulders (three times)
   c) Push forwards to the front, then back (three times)
   Relax; repeat three to five times.
2 **Arm raises** Another exercise is to raise the arms to shoulder height out sideways, swing them round to the right as far as possible three times, then back to centre. Repeat on the opposite side; relax. Repeat three times each way. This exercise will help to loosen the waist and improve balance. Make sure the rider remains central in the saddle and keeps a secure leg position.

● BELOW: *Pulling the legs up and doing arm exercises increases balance and co-ordination, as well as loosening the arms and shoulders. It is not so easy as it looks!*

● BOTTOM LEFT: *'Round the World' is a popular exercise requiring suppleness, balance and co-ordination. Make sure you raise your leg high enough over the horse's rump to avoid hitting his back. Always have a helper to hold the horse*

1

2

3

4

1 *Raising the arms helps to improve balance and co-ordination as well as stretching the back and waist. The arms can swing together or go in different directions in circular movements. This is also the start position for bending and touching toes*

2 *This is the starting position for most of the arm exercises. If real benefit is to be achieved it is important to keep the shoulders low and loose and not let them get tight. From this position the arms can then go up or forwards or rotate backwards – all movements which help to loosen shoulders, elbows and wrists*

3 *In this exercise both arms are held out to the side and then the rider swings round as far as possible to one side and then the other. This helps to loosen arms, shoulders, back and waist*

4 *Arm swings are useful exercises to improve balance, suppleness and co-ordination. Always ensure you have a helper to hold the horse if doing these mounted. This exercise has many variations which can be done – they can also be done unmounted. In this picture the rider has both hands out to the sides and is swinging each arm back and forward which helps to loosen the shoulders*

3 Backwards bend Whilst the leg must remain gently secure against the horse, the rider should relax the upper body sufficiently to lie back on to the horse's rump; then sit up again. It is essential that a handler holds the horse. Never do this more than three times.

4 Forwards stretch Raise one arm above the head and bend forwards and down as far as possible to touch the foot on the opposite side; then return to the starting position. Relax. Repeat on the other side. This could be done up to three times, one each side. A handler must hold the horse.

● *Crossing the hands behind the back and pulling back the shoulders is a good loosening exercise. Just getting the arms in position is not easy*

● *Leaning back on the horse's back is a great favourite with children. It is excellent for improving the suppleness of the back. This exercise should only be done with a quiet horse and with a saddle that has a low cantle*

● *Bending forwards to touch the toes requires quite an effort. The exercise starts with the arms raised up above the head, and then the rider bends forwards touching the left toe with the right arm – to return to the upright position and repeat with the opposite arm*

Exercises When Moving

Riding without stirrups This is undoubtedly the most effective riding exercise to make a rider concentrate on the correct, erect but supple position in the saddle. It is one practised regularly by all riders, from beginner to Olympic standard. To start with it should be done on the lunge line, and always with beginners; cross the stirrups over the wither in front of the saddle or remove them altogether. Adjust the position if necessary to sit centrally in the saddle, remembering to grow tall from the waist upwards; sit as softly as possible, but deep into the saddle, feeling the weight evenly on both seatbones. Relax into the movement of the horse, and allow the body to move *with* the horse rather than against it.

Start at walk, and progress to trot and canter. The trainer should watch the rider's position, particularly during transitions from one pace to another when it is very easy for bad habits to materialise. Keep in balance with the horse, and do not allow the weight to tip either forwards or too far back; be sure to keep the legs lightly secure against the horse's sides, rather than allowing them to flop backwards or forwards.

The hands must not control balance by gripping on the reins, but must remain soft and independent. If the rider is being lunged he can forget about the reins, which can be knotted up or looped round the neck and the horse lunged with side-reins. This enables the rider to progress to doing arm exercises on the lunge without stirrups.

Arm exercises when done without stirrups can be very useful for improving balance and confidence; they also help to ensure the rider uses his legs more effectively to influence the horse to increase or decrease pace. Arm exercises can be performed at walk, trot or canter depending on the rider's

● *Leg exercises help to settle the rider into the saddle and stretch and loosen all parts of the leg, as well as the hip, knee and ankle joints. Sit centrally in the saddle and use the pommel as a balancing aid but do not pull on this. Swing your legs forwards and backwards and outwards or upwards. Rotate the feet in both directions to loosen the ankle joint*

experience. Raise the arms to shoulder height and stretch out to the sides; continue with the same arm routine as in the stationary exercises. Continue to alternate arm swings, with one arm swinging forwards and the other back in slow, steady circular swings – this is not as easy as it sounds!

Another exercise is to swing both arms backwards in a slow, circular movement; then reverse this, and swing forwards. Remember all the time to keep your weight central and in balance with the horse. One of the main faults to guard against when riding without stirrups is that of gripping upwards which will push you up out of the saddle – you should relax the hips so as to sink down into the saddle, allowing the legs to stretch down as far as possible. The knee should remain close to the saddle without tightening, but the lower calf should be as taut as is necessary against the horse's side, with the heel vibrating against the horse's sides to encourage it forwards or just to hold it firmly together between hand and leg.

Riding without stirrups can be extremely helpful. A change in saddle type can sometimes make quite a difference to rider style and comfort, especially if he has tended to get too far backwards in perhaps a jumping saddle. By riding without stirrups or in the straighter-cut dressage saddle it is possible that a whole new feel and awareness is experienced of what a correct position should be. Once a rider has felt the right feel it is much easier to achieve again, even if in a less helpfully shaped saddle.

Rising trot without stirrups This is quite strenuous and should only be practised for a short time. It will help to strengthen the thigh muscles and inner knee for those who find it difficult to grip with the knees. Its main purpose is to increase versatility and strength rather than to improve riding as such, but all riders should be able to do this without too much effort once they have become reasonably competent. To start with, try three or four strides; then relax. As this exercise is best practised on the straight rather than on a circle and is therefore best done off the lunge, make sure the horse does not look worried during its execution.

● *Leg pulls help to stretch and tone the leg muscles particularly the thigh; they also improve balance*

● *Exercises at trot and canter on the lunge without reins or stirrups are excellent for balance*

● *Arm exercises can be done on the lunge and will help with co-ordination and balance. The trainer watches what happens to the leg position when other parts of the body are doing different exercises*

General Health Assessment

Practising all these exercises should give you some idea as to whether you are fit enough to progress with your riding or not. Most basically fit people find little problem apart from slight stiffness if they have overdone things. However, the complete beginner who is not accustomed to much physical exertion may find it more difficult, especially if he has done little in the way of walking, running, swimming, cycling or general exercise routines.

At this stage it is therefore just as well to reassess progress, and in particular to ensure that you have the right equipment and are not getting sore or rubbed – trying to avoid sensitive areas can quickly lead to bad habits. Don't be a martyr if you are getting a sore backside or knees – have a day or two off, and use a skin hardener such as surgical spirit (rubbing alcohol) if the skin is unbroken, followed by powder. Be sure to use more padding over these areas, either in

● *Traditional chaps are comfortable, protect the leg and can be quickly unzipped when off the horse*

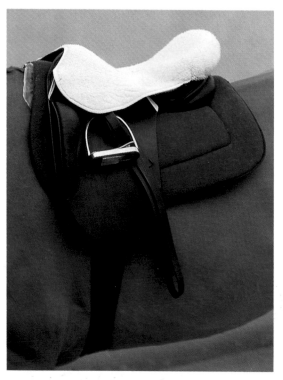

● *The seat saver is an excellent aid for those who tend to get sore in the saddle. It is also helpful for those who have back problems as it absorbs some of the jarring effect suffered by a rider who is tense in the saddle*

the form of thicker breeches or jodhpurs, or heavier tights underneath; and never be too proud to use a 'seat saver' on your saddle, or to put a spare numnah (saddle pad) over the top of your saddle to make it softer. Skinny people, and men in particular with their narrower hips, often suffer from this problem. Sometimes the stirrup leathers cause pinched calves, although with proper breeches and boots, or tougher jodhpurs, or by using chaps this can usually be prevented.

General stiffness is bound to occur at some stage, however careful you are, but there are many remedies aimed at its relief. It is usually at its worst in cold weather, as one tends to tighten already tired muscles against the cold thus compounding the problem. An old-fashioned remedy which I have always found extremely beneficial is to put one tablespoon of mustard powder into a hot bath. You will emerge rather a strange colour and tingling all over, but with all traces of stiffness completely gone; however, I do not recommend this in the summer or in hot weather when a good dip in a pool will probably be a better way to loosen up stiff muscles. Jacuzzis are also highly recommended, but do not stay in for too long.

For more advanced work there is no substitute for riding more often and more intensely, making yourself work that little bit harder and longer so as to achieve success – you hope! – with greater ease. The sitting trot without stirrups could go on for longer, and you could do canter work in the same way. Schooling the horse under the watchful eye of your trainer will enable you to concentrate your attention on what you are doing, and he will definitely keep you hard at it until results are achieved – on your own it is often too easy to give up when you start to ache. However, as you progress, so you must push yourself that bit more, to be sure that your fitness and capabilities really do improve. It is also a good idea to ride different horses, as this will prevent you from becoming a 'one horse rider', and will help to build that other vital ingredient which you

will need besides fitness for success: experience. Every horse requires a different approach and you will have to adjust to this, finding out for yourself how to cope with such factors as variation in temperament, striding, standard of training. The more you do and the greater your awareness, the more capable you will be at coping with whatever comes your way.

As you ride more, you will be able to cut down on the other fitness exercises you might be doing. For example, if you are riding every day, it should not be necessary to do other exercises at all unless you feel the need; but if you only ride at weekends, one or two workouts during the week would certainly be beneficial.

● *The end of a training session. These two riders have done a swap onto each other's horses and so look a little over- and under-horsed. The size of the horse can make a big difference as to how effective the rider is when schooling*

Falls and Injuries

Inevitably there will be times when the rider has a fall, and no serious horseman escapes this experience! Regardless of how good he may be, there will always be the unexpected lurking round the corner which may cause the horse to react suddenly; or the rider might make an error of judgement which results in a fall. Whatever the reason, the golden rule is to relax and if possible to roll away from the horse, thereby minimising the risk of injury; though of course this is much easier said than done, and until you have actually experienced a fall you will hardly know what to expect. Nevertheless each fall (if you are unlucky enough to have more than a few!) will help develop your sense of self-preservation, and there is no doubt that your reflexes become much more acute and you learn how to react quickly enough to stay on. The best advice is: if in doubt, sit up!

● *Disaster – the point of no return! It should be possible with most falls to try to curl up as you land, and roll away from the horse to minimise the risk of injury*

Bruising is, of course, the normal result of any fall, and in 90 per cent of cases this will be the worst that will happen – although one's pride may have taken a serious blow! In these times when herbal health is very much back in favour, *arnica* is the rider's best friend and should be in every first-aid cupboard. Taken straightaway, its powerful healing properties soon remove any sign or symptom of bruising, as long as the follow-up doses are taken as prescribed. There are many other remedies, too: ice on a bad bruise applied immediately to the injured area will help to prevent further bruising, and in many cases will have a dramatic effect. Never forget that the application of something cold is essential first-aid treatment to prevent bruising becoming more serious; if nothing else is immediately available, take a packet of frozen peas or chips out of the freezer whilst other remedies are being prepared.

The injuries most often incurred as a result of riding falls are to the head and neck, including concussion; to the back; and broken bones of which collar bones (clavicle), ankles and wrists are perhaps the most common. Every stable should have the

doctor's and the vet's numbers' by the telephone, and a simple but complete first-aid kit readily available. (For guidance on how to deal with injuries, see p167.) The best preventative is, however, never to take risks: riding is certainly to be enjoyed, but those who take unnecessary risks really only have themselves to blame. Follow the advice of more experienced people, and avoid the more obvious pitfalls by remembering some of riding's golden rules:

1   Think ahead – horses are sometimes quick-thinking and generally have quick reactions, and they can be easily frightened.
2   Do not take risks, especially with children or inexperienced riders.
3   Remember that young children and even your own, heretofore reliable horses/-ponies can be unpredictable and react irrationally.
4   Never overdo any exercise or jump.
5   Keep all tack and equipment in good condition.
6   Ensure that the horse's feet and legs are kept in good shape.
7   Riding or jumping at excessive speed is dangerous.
8   Keep children away from unknown horses or ponies.
9   Never forget that horses and ponies are stronger than you, and need firm but kind handling.
10 Learn to understand your horse so that he trusts you.

Specialising: the Different Disciplines

At some stage a rider will probably come to the conclusion that he finds one aspect of riding particularly attractive, and will decide to take it up more seriously. There are several disciplines to choose from, so there should be something to appeal to every type of personality, from the more timid to those who like to live dangerously. Perhaps a trekking holiday initiated the enthusiasm for riding; some may have helped at riding schools, or watched enviously as friends rode by in obvious enjoyment. Going to an event may have fired the imagination of an already horse-mad enthusiast.

Whatever the reason, the horse is a most magnificent and genuine animal, and it has an amazing effect on those already favourably motivated. Riders who are ambitious soon develop a competitive instinct once they have mastered the basic skills, and it is usually not long before the appeal of the various disciplines are more thoroughly scrutinised.

There is, of course, something for everyone. Trekking through beautiful countryside is perhaps the most leisurely form of riding, though never underestimate how stiff and tired you might become, not to mention how sore you may feel if you do not prepare yourself adequately. Long distance riding is a more competitive and strenuous extension of trekking: at top level it demands the highest degree of horsemastership and horsemanship if both horse and rider are to complete the different stages in peak condition. Rides from twenty-five to a hundred miles are the most common, and the rider must have a sound knowledge of how to monitor progress in the fitness required for the different levels.

Western riding is fast gaining support in the British Isles, and is already, of course, immensely popular in the States. A high degree of training is required, firstly in the classical style and then more particularly in neck reining and specialist movements such as turns, sliding stops, spins, pivots, roll-backs and flying changes, all performed in Western clothing and tack.

The more competitive rider may find that pure show jumping or eventing suit him better. For those more interested in the basics of training, pure dressage will be the answer, whether building up their schooling routine to reach the very top, even Grand Prix level, or just working at the lower levels.

The elegance of side-saddle riding appeals to thousands, as is amply proved by the enormous number of classes now provided for the side-saddle rider, with everything from equitation classes to working hunters and jumping.

● Barrel racing is one of the most popular of the Western riding sports. The design of the Western saddle encourages a longer style of riding with a generally looser rein contact
● Hacking out provides exercise, companionship and a great feeling of well being

Voltige (vaulting), so popular on the Continent, involves young people early on, and the skills required must stand them in good stead should they progress to conventional riding disciplines at a later stage. The tremendous timing, poise and co-ordination which it requires, not to mention that important word 'balance', are all of inestimable value when it comes to more conventional riding. In Europe, voltige is almost universally considered the ideal start for riders; perhaps the deep continental seat stems from this excellent foundation.

Other sports have equally great support: for example, polo; and racing either on the flat or over fences, which may ideally suit the athletic shorter person. The seasonal increase in riders during the hunting months testifies to the huge popularity of this sport; it has also proved an invaluable training ground for top performance horses and riders.

For the more all-round sportsperson, tetrathlon and pentathlon could be a great incentive – the fun (and hard work) of training for several athletic and sporting skills certainly has its appeal amongst the younger generation. (For advice on specialist fitness training for these various different equestrian activities, see p128.)

Suitability of Horse and Rider for a Chosen Sport

If you want to succeed or at least participate in a particular discipline with some degree of success, it is important that your horse is of the right type for the work you are expecting him to do. For instance, it would be hopeless to expect a Shire horse to compete in a three-day event or a thoroughbred in a ploughing contest. Likewise the rider should be able to perform adequately within his limits if he is to gain satisfaction from what he has set out to achieve. For example, a five-foot rider is unlikely to be able to get the best out of a 17hh horse and such a partnership might be dangerously out of control in, say, a horse trial or out hunting – the horse would simply be too big for the rider.

The weight of the rider can make an enormous difference to the effectiveness of his demands, and it is a basic requirement that the competitive rider keeps himself fit and within the average weight bracket for his height and frame. No one can really ride at his best unless he is of a reasonable size – although many larger people are perfectly happy pacing themselves to perform very adequately within their limits.

Some horses seem tailor-made for certain activities, and this is not necessarily determined by type or breeding but more by temperament and character. It really is very often a case of trial and error – sometimes you discover that your little wonder has no intention of turning into the star role you had in mind for it, at others the horse with the most unlikely credentials turns out to have those hidden qualities which come out when you least expect it. Certain horses are hopeless at one thing, but turn out to be brilliant at another. Others will go exceptionally well for one rider and not a yard for another – so you can never be 100 per cent sure that you have what you think you have anyway!

If you are going to look at a new horse, always take an experienced person with you, and never forget that it has to be right for *you* – in size, temperament and ability, for what you have in mind – not everyone else! You might find it too big or too strong, too small or excitable: before you make any decision, therefore, you must be sure you feel quite happy with it, and should try it out thoroughly both by yourself and with others. Do not forget that being shown a horse in an unfit state is a classic dealer's trick when trying to sell something that tends to hot up

---

● LEFT: *Vaulting or voltige is increasing in popularity in Britain and America. Always a favourite in Europe, this is a wonderful way of improving timing, balance and co-ordination as well as fostering an awareness of the movement of the horse*
● OVERLEAF: *Polo is a very strenuous sport requiring fitness and balance from both horse and rider*

● Side-saddle riding can be taken up
at an early age. It requires balance
but is relatively easy thanks to the
design of the saddle

● *The suitability of the horse to the rider is important. This young jockey appears over-horsed, however, the smile indicates that all is well. A horse that is not too strong and has a good temperament is perfectly suitable, whereas one that is a puller could be disastrous*

and get strong when fit; so particularly if you are a beginner or inexperienced, try to discuss it with a previous owner or someone who has known the horse other than the person selling. It must also, of course, pass the vet, who can assess its physical fitness for the job you have in mind before any transaction takes place and before you take it on. This really is worthwhile, as it is the only safeguard you have that at least it was passed as physically suitable on the date vetted; the vet's certificate can then be used by the insurance company, as long as you arrange this at the same time and send off the details immediately.

● *This jockey is under-horsed – the pony is too small for the size of the rider. Although amazingly strong for their size, ponies cannot be expected to jump or gallop safely if they have a rider too large for them*

3 EQUINE HEALTH & FITNESS

● *The health and well-being of the horse is clear here. The bright eye, rounded outline, glossy coat and generally interested appearance are the most obvious signs of good health*

The fitness of the horse is determined by its general health and well-being, and its steady preparation to peak physical condition so it can cope easily with the demands placed upon it. In the final weeks a horse's training programme will differ according to the activity it is being trained for, but the basic requirements for general fitness are broadly similar. However, no animal can be prepared for any role without first enjoying proper basic care in the form of good horse management, whether it is to be ridden at weekends only or aimed for a top competitive career. It is vital, therefore, to appreciate the importance of basic care in relation to fitness.

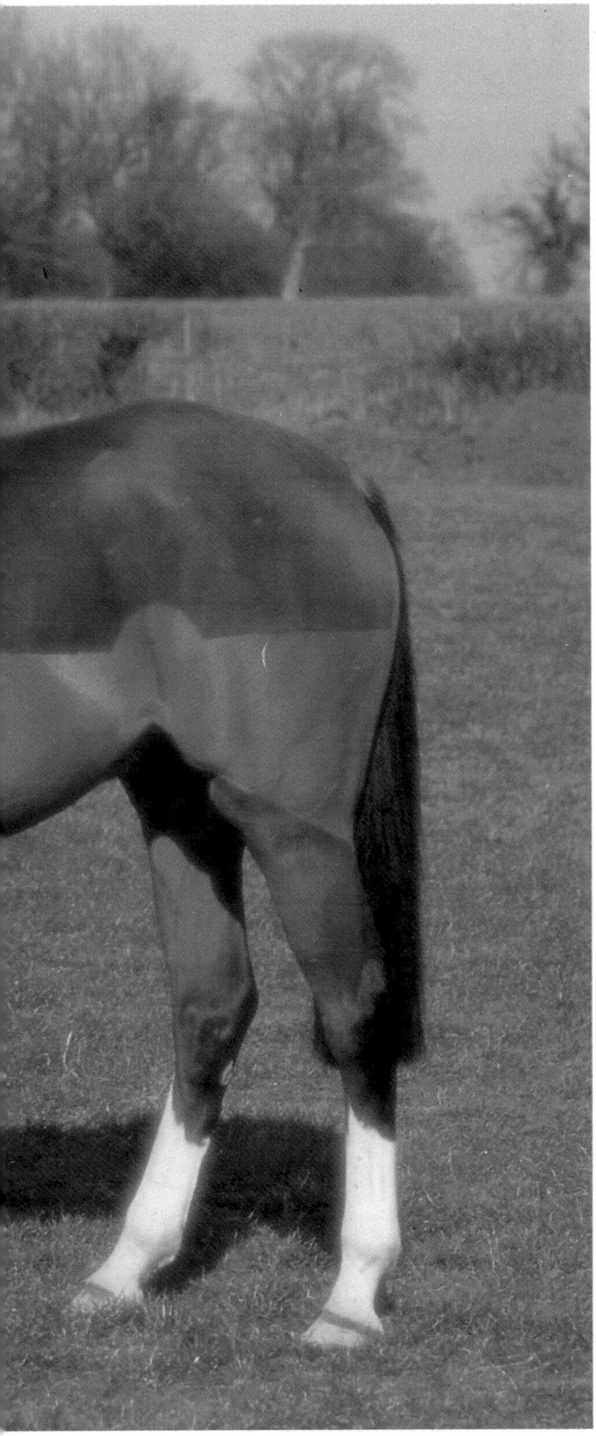

The Healthy Horse

The first and obvious signs of health in the horse are a bright eye and a glossy coat, although the condition of the coat will obviously depend on the type of animal and the time of year, and whether it is stabled or out at grass. However, the feel of the skin should be loose and supple, and the horse should present an overall picture of health. Its temperature, pulse and respiration (TPR) are the next most important indications of its physical well-being, and these should always be assessed when the animal is quiet and resting. When monitoring fitness this should be done at the same time each day if a true picture is to be obtained. It is essential that every horse owner knows what constitutes 'normal' for the horse; the following chart indicates 'normal' readings and the effect exercise can have on these.

	Temperature	Pulse Beats per minute	Respiration Breaths per minute
Normal	37.5°–38°C	35–40	8–15
Following moderate exercise	38°–39°C	40–120	40–70
Following heavy exercise	39°–40°C	120–200	70–100

Weather conditions, duration of work, fitness levels and temperament will all play a significant role in the above readings. The pulse and respiration levels will drop quickly (once work ceases) over the following five to ten minutes, and should be near normal after twenty to thirty minutes.

Respiration rates may remain high for longer in very hot/humid conditions. Any readings above those indicated in the bottom line will require prompt veterinary attention to reduce the levels before long-term damage is done to the horse.

If at any time the horse does not appear well or itself, its temperature should be taken; this is done rectally, and the thermometer should be held whilst inserted for the specified time (usually one to two minutes). The normal horse temperature is 37.5° to 38°C (100–100.5°F); the youngster or foal may be slightly higher.

The pulse should be taken when the horse is quiet, and is easily felt where the artery passes over the jawbone; it should be around thirty-five to forty beats a minute, which again may be higher in youngsters. Sensitive horses, like humans, will react to excitement or stress with a raised pulse, so this sort must be well settled to get a true reading.

The normal rate of respiration should be between eight to fifteen breaths a minute; it is read by watching the horse's flanks and the visible movement of the ribs as it breathes.

A horse in good condition will have a pleasing, rounded shape; he will be neither too fat, as he will not then be able to perform easily, and it will put strain on certain organs; nor must he be too thin. A good basic guide is to assess the muscles of the top line of the horse: these should be rounded, and the horse must not look unduly angular for its type; similarly if you can feel, rather than see the ribs and the hip bones, and if the overall picture looks healthy rather than too fat or too thin, then your horse is probably within the 'about right' category.

● TOP RIGHT: *This horse is looking fat following a summer out at grass – it would not be able to perform any strenuous exercise in this state without the risk of damage to legs, heart and wind. Fat tends to build up inside the horse as well as externally in the areas indicated*

● BELOW RIGHT: *This young horse looks rather lean and fit and, although not really thin, is not carrying much extra flesh. When horses are in poor condition they tend to lose muscle and excess fat first after which the ribs, hipbones, shoulders and spine become more obvious. The belly will be drawn up as the horse loses condition and the coat will lose its gloss. A horse in peak fitness will also have a drawn-up appearance but should have muscle on top, along its neck, spine and quarters, with a glossy coat and a general appearance of health and well-being*

● BELOW: *Finding the horse's pulse is most easily achieved by pressing the artery that runs in the jaw groove against the bone as indicated. The resting pulse is around 35-40 beats a minute*

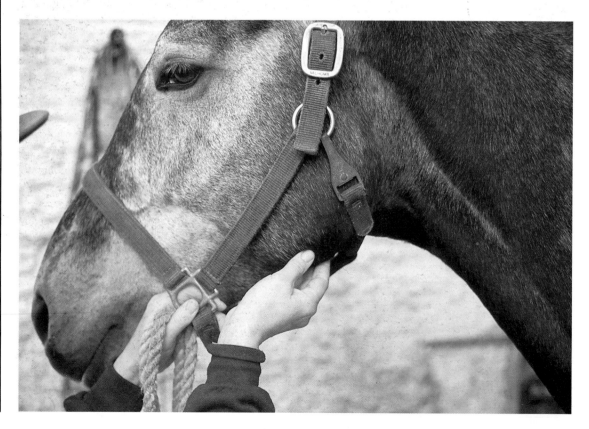

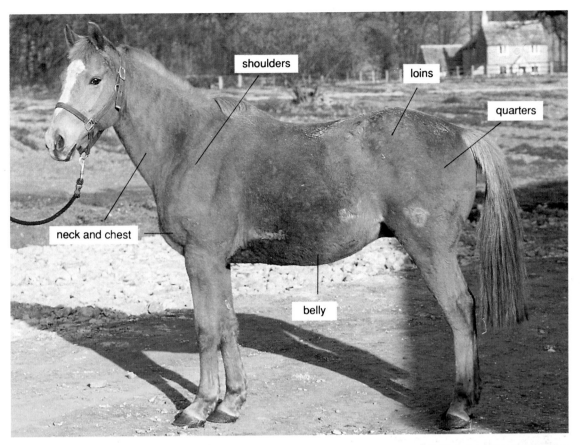

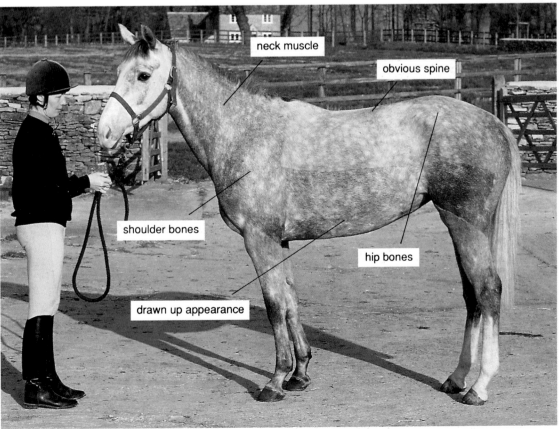

A horse's ears are often a good guide to its general well-being; they should be alert and enquiring, and should confirm the horse's whole outlook which should be cheerful and interested. A dull and listless demeanour will indicate lack of health and should be investigated. Generally a horse's ears are pricked forward when he is interested in what is going on, for example when out hacking or at feed times; they are laid back when he is cross, or being obstinate, or if he is frightened; and they may flick backwards and forwards if he is worried or concentrating. The ears are therefore one of our few means of telling what a horse is thinking or feeling, and the discerning owner can learn a lot by watching and interpreting from them the horse's physical and mental state.

The limbs should be clean, with ligaments and tendons well defined; there should be no signs of undue filling, and they should feel the same temperature. In general they should feel cool, but this will depend on the time of day, how hot the weather is, how much work the horse has done, and his state of fitness at the time. The feet, so vital to the working horse, must be in good condition and shape. If they become out of balance this could have a detrimental effect on the whole animal, which if worked in this state could go lame.

The horse's appetite is a good indication of health, and most healthy horses eat well so long as their teeth have been regularly checked and rasped. Failure to do this can make it extremely uncomfortable for the horse, as uneven edges form on his teeth causing soreness and irritation; in severe cases these can significantly restrict his ability to chew his food properly. Teeth should be rasped at least once a year, and checked every six months.

The droppings will indicate the type of food the horse has been having: in the stabled horse they will be drier and a deep golden-brownish colour; those of the grass-kept animal will probably be greener in colour. The horse may defecate twelve to twenty-five times a day, and any changes in his normal droppings – for example their consistency, or odour not related to the diet – should be noted. Note that excitement or stress may have a definite effect on some animals, and cause their droppings to be loose; dry feed may sometimes help in these cases. Wet or damp feeding, with added oil, may help those horses prone to dry or constipated droppings.

The urine is indicative of the amount a horse drinks; generally he will drink between six to ten gallons a day, although hot weather and travelling may increase this considerably as a result of dehydration and body metabolism. Urine will be more concentrated in the mornings after the horse has rested, but is generally a pale straw colour. Any change in its normal colour should be reported at once to the vet, especially if it becomes very dark brown or bloodstained; this might indicate infection or muscle damage, and early diagnoses will help to prevent complications developing. It must be stressed that such a condition is relatively rare.

It is most important to get to know and understand the horse well so that you know what is normal for that particular horse. How he looks, how he reacts and how he copes are characteristics which you need to know so you can identify what is normal and what is abnormal for that particular animal should problems arise.

If you are ever worried, always check temperature and pulse, and watch his respiration. If these do not indicate much difference but you still know something is wrong, call your vet – and always call him if the horse has a temperature so that he can deal with any problem before it gets out of hand. Later is often too late.

● *Alert youngsters waiting for their daily exercise. If the young are given a good start in life they should grow and thrive and reach their true potential. Regular worming, feet care and good food, as well as proper handling all help to create a mutual respect which should pay off when these yearlings come to be broken in as three-year-olds*

General Care

The horse must be checked every day whether he is stabled or out at grass. Look to see that he is sound, has no abnormal lumps or bumps, and that he is well in himself. Make sure you see the grass-kept horse move if you are not riding him, so you know he is sound. Get into the habit of noticing expression, legs and general stance as a matter of course – a good horsemaster has only to walk into a yard and he will see straightaway if a horse is not right by the way it is looking or standing.

A horse will only be as fit as you make him through a correct combination of feeding, exercise and gradual build-up. Plan your training schedule so that you reach peak fitness for whatever you are aiming for with about a week in hand to cover any slight set-backs. Remember, the golden rule is to 'make haste slowly', and never be tempted to rush the all-important period of slow conditioning work that precedes all training. It is also wise to examine the different health aspects of horse management and the reasons why future performance might be affected if any one is neglected.

Teeth

All too often the annual dental check is neglected because the horse is 'eating well'. Teeth should be rasped by your horse dentist or vet once a year *at least*, to ensure that the hooks and sharp edges that inevitably appear through uneven mastication of food do not build up to uncomfortable proportions. Watch your horse eating and look to see if he is having difficulty with chewing in any way, or appears to be trying to eat on one side of his mouth. Messy eating habits are sometimes caused by the horse trying to avoid a certain part of his mouth – although some horses are simply just messy!

● *The tooth rasp is especially designed to give an even surface to the teeth. A special gag is often used to aid this procedure which most horses accept quite happily*

How to Feel your Horse's Teeth

It requires a specialist with a proper equine gag to keep the horse's mouth open sufficiently and for long enough to examine its teeth properly, but the horse owner can get a very good indication of their general state by having a quick feel himself. Firstly put one hand on his nose, then slip the fingers of the other into the side of his mouth and gently but firmly take hold of the tongue and bring it out to the side. *Make sure you have a safe hold of this*, then put your fingers, keeping them flat, into the mouth on the opposite side to that from which you have taken the tongue. Run your fingers up the outside and inside of the teeth along both the top and bottom jaws. Repeat the performance on the other side, always remembering the importance of keeping the tongue well out to the side if you want to retain fingers and hand in one piece!

● *Checking a horse's teeth: pull the tongue gently out to one side, and then feel up the line of lower and upper teeth on the other side. Teeth should be rasped at least once a year to ensure even wear. Teeth problems not only prevent the horse from masticating his food correctly but can also be the cause of numerous bitting problems*

The sharpness of the hooks which can develop on teeth is often surprising, and it is understandable how these can cause great discomfort to the horse. The bit and noseband could well add to this discomfort, especially a grakle (figure eight) or flash noseband which might press against one of these sore areas, and this could well be the reason why a horse is a one-sider, or shakes his head, or leans on the bit. Remember that teeth care is essential for good health, and if your horse does not look great, then they should always be checked first before you resort to any of the numerous remedies on the market.

Worming

Another important priority is a regular worming routine. All horses have some worms, but regular worming should keep these under control. Before the days of sprays and pesticides, horses were able to keep themselves reasonably well by eating a variety of plants and herbs, many of which had anti-worm properties. The old stud grooms used to 'purge' horses with various herb-based potions, and give them a 'physic' twice a year; nowadays, however, there are effective wormers on the market which we know need to be given regularly, alternating the different market brands.

● *Regular worming is essential to the horse's health. Doses can be given in pellet form in the feed, or via paste in a syringe inserted in the corner of the mouth, as shown*

Discuss your worming routine with your vet, and follow it conscientiously. It may be a good idea to get a worm sample taken from your horse's droppings, especially if he is showing any of the classic symptoms of the worm-infested horse – these include a harsh stary coat, loss of condition, a pot-belly appearance, tail-rubbing, coughing which often indicates lungworm, and loose smelly droppings which may or may not show the presence of worms. Land management is essential if this problem is not to continue, especially if you have only a small paddock (see Chapter 4).

Feeding

The types and amounts of food given to the horse should be carefully assessed, especially if you intend to work him hard and are expecting a continued standard of performance. The amounts given will depend on how much work he is doing, his age, temperament and his overall condition. Feed little and often and stick to regular meal-times. Water must always be freely available, and another bucket should be provided or more regular checks made in hot weather to ensure the horse does not go short in these conditions. When a horse is to be stabled having been out at grass he should not be put on a crash diet.

Never skimp on quality; your horse needs the best hay and food available. The mixture of bulk foods and concentrates should always be such that there is never less than 50 per cent bulk (roughage) in his diet, although this is sometimes reduced further with, for example, racehorses, or eventers which must be more finely tuned. Make sure your food is fresh – all feed comes with a date stamp which guarantees that its nutritional qualities will remain if stored adequately until that date.

The horse should not be fed immediately after work, nor just before it is ridden – at least an hour should be allowed for it to settle and digest its food. If competing or doing fast work it should not eat for two to four hours beforehand.

As a general rule, be sure you feed according to the work being done. If you run out of time or do not give your horse the work you feel he should be having, or he stays in for any reason, you must cut down on the food intake. If necessary just give some Mollichop without the concentrates, a bran mash, or if the horse is fat, give half the normal quantity – but whatever you do, cut it down.

Types of Feed

The following are the most important and common feeds fed to horses:

Oats are the most important part of the horse's diet and if of good quality provide an adequate amount of protein. Traditionally these have always been the food of choice, but they do tend to have a 'heating' effect on some animals, making them rather over-excitable if care is not taken. In this case either cut down on the quantity or change to feeding barley which is generally less likely to have this effect. Oats are best fed bruised, but can also be fed boiled when they are more easily digestible; this is excellent for those rather out of condition.

Barley is becoming the food of choice for many, having a higher energy content than

● *There are many different types of feed: chaff, cubes, mix, corn and sugar beet pellets (before and after soaking) are shown here. It is vital that sugar beet is thoroughly soaked for 12 to 24 hours before being fed as it swells to up to five times when wet*

oats; it is usually fed rolled or micronised. It is also excellent boiled and usually makes up the bulk of a boiled mix. Although unexplained scientifically, barley does seem to be less heating than oats. Both foods have a poor calcium-to-phosphorous ratio, and if fed without much other fodder except hay, will need a suitable supplement to correct this imbalance.

Maize (corn) is used less now than it used to be, but it is high in energy and is fed either flaked or micronised. It is to be found in many of the mixes where its golden and crisp appearance is very noticeable.

Peas and beans are to be found mainly in the coarse mixes (sweet feed). They have a high energy and protein content but can have the affect of being 'heating'.

Linseed is produced from the flax plant and is high in energy and fat. It must be cooked, and is fed either as jelly, or the seeds are often mixed with barley or oats as boiled feed. It is excellent used like this with a bran mash, and its high oil content helps to keep the skin and coat in good condition.

Sugar-beet pulp has a high energy content and is easily digested. It must be carefully soaked, probably overnight (though in cold conditions when the water is likely to freeze you may have to leave it longer – or bring the bucket into the house) and all users of sugar-beet must realise the dangers of not soaking it correctly. The pulp or pellets will expand dramatically in water, and one level scoop of sugar-beet should be added to at least three-quarters of a bucket of water and left for at least twelve hours. There have been occasional tragic cases of animals being fed the pellets dry; these have then expanded inside the stomach, which ruptures with fatal results. Choking can also occur with dry pulp. Always ensure sugar-beet is stored separately from other pellets, and that everyone is aware of what it is, and how it should be used. It has a high calcium-to-phosphorus value, therefore if fed with cereals it will help to correct the imbalance in the diet.

Bran is derived from the inner wheat husk and is a filler with little nutritional value; it is traditionally used for making a bran mash. It has slightly laxative qualities when fed wet, and has a binding effect if fed dry. Good quality broad bran should have obvious flakes, but all too often this sort is hard to find.

Because of its detrimental effect on calcium uptake, bran is used far less than in the past apart from the weekly bran mash; if used extensively, a calcium supplement should be used.

Chaff or **Mollichop** was traditionally a mixture of chopped hay and straw, but nowadays this has tended to be mixed with molasses making it a more palatable and nutritional filler. The horse requires a balance between roughage and cereals and this is one of the most popular means of adding roughage to the diet. It has also been marketed with added herbs such as comfrey and garlic.

Compound feeds are those feeds that have been formulated to provide a balanced ration for the horse. They generally come in two main forms, cubes (pellets) and mixes (sweet feeds).

The cubes may be designed as a complete ration, or they may have to be used with other cereals and roughage to produce a balanced feed. Coarse mixes consist of a combination of different foods which make up a balanced ration. Generally both cubes and mixes will have had mineral and vitamin additions to balance the diet. They should also state clearly what the protein content is, and it is best to start with the lowest percentage until you feel your horse may need more: 9 to 11 per cent protein is generally found in the 'Horse and Pony' mixes or cubes, whereas 16 to 22 per cent may be found in stud or racehorse cubes. In general if the horse is looking and feeling well, do not go for higher protein but keep your horse happy on the lower levels. There are far more problems caused by over-feeding than by under-feeding.

Hay provides the necessary bulk and roughage in the stabled horse's diet, as grass does to animals out in the field; being dried grass, hay is the food nearest to the horse's natural diet. There are two main types of hay: meadow and seed. It is essential for good health that any hay is well made and is not dusty; moreover, it will only be as good as the ground from which it has been grown. Generally hay is not eaten until the new year after it was made; it is at its best between six to eighteen months after making, after which its nutritional value diminishes.

● *Good hay should smell sweet and fresh. Dusty or mouldy hay should never be used. Hay is at its best 6 to 18 months after being made*

When introducing new hay do so gradually in case it upsets the horse's stomach, particularly if it is new hay. Perhaps start by adding the new at night and the old in the morning, or some similar system, over a three- to four-day period.

Meadow hay is generally softer, being cut from permanent pasture; it therefore contains a variety of grasses, herbs and vetches, although its protein value may vary depending on where the grass is situated.

Seed hay is purpose-grown with a pre-prepared seed mixture and may include such grasses as timothy, rye, lucerne (alfalfa), clover. It is generally higher in feed value, but the really stiff, stalky variety is not as popular with the horse.

If your horse suffers from a dust allergy or coughs after eating hay, he should be fed soaked hay or tried on Horsehage, a vacuum-packed hay mixture.

Silage for horses is becoming more popular, but care must be taken as regards quality and the method of making it – it is best to ask the advice of those who feed it, and find out any particular problems. Generally it is all right if made in its own juices, but on many farms additives are added to the bales; these may not all be suitable, so it is important to check that all ingredients are acceptable for horses. Silage should be introduced to the diet gradually.

Succulents in the form of apples, carrots and root vegetables add variation to the diet and are generally enjoyed by the horse.

Cod liver oil is good for the coat and looseness of the skin as well as being useful in helping resistance to infections. Oil is particularly useful in cold weather and when the horse 'goes off' a bit, such as when changing his coat.

● *Well-made hay is one of the stabled horse's most important foods. If your horse has a dust allergy, or coughs, he may be best fed soaked hay. Various methods of soaking and draining hay are shown here. Hay should be soaked for at least 12 hours so that the spores expand sufficiently and are not ingested*

Salt should be freely available to the horse in the form of a salt lick, or a dessertspoonful (US tbs) can be added to the food in hot weather. Most compound foods or mixes already have salt in the right quantities in their formulas.

Eggs some people like to add eggs, which are rich in protein, to the diet; if the horse likes them, there is no reason why he should not have a couple a day. (NB *In the USA the feeding of raw eggs to horses is not recommended because of the risk of salmonella poisoning.*)

Beer is an excellent pick-me-up, and if enjoyed could be given to an off-colour horse.

Herbs

The use of herbs has become very fashionable both for human and horse, and many horses are known to have derived benefit from the use of certain herbs when other more orthodox remedies have failed. Certainly I have experienced great benefit from herbal medicine myself and I have also noticed the improvement with some horses. Like us, however, animals are individuals and what works with one may not have the same effect with another.

Herbal Medicine for Horses

The use of plants to help the process of healing is the oldest order of medicine in the world. Complex and sophisticated systems of herbal medicine existed in the Far East 3,000 years ago, and written records of herbal remedies have been found in Egypt dating from about 1,500 BC.

The present-day herbalist uses the whole plant, fresh or dried, and prepared in a variety of ways: as an infusion (teas); as tinctures and liquid extracts, for poultices; as tablets; or creams and ointments. The key factor is the use of the whole plant. Unlike a pharmaceutical scientist, the herbalist does not isolate certain active principles from a plant; moreover, using the entire plant probably accounts for the fact that side-effects

from the use of herbal remedies are comparatively rare. The very substances which pharmaceutical laboratories discard as impurities in fact balance and complement the medicinal action.

The wild animal will fast itself until restored to health, partaking only of water and certain medicinal herbs which it will seek out instinctively for a cure of the malady from which it is suffering. Sadly, our horses generally miss out on grazing time because of their domesticated lifestyle, and anyway pastures are often cleared of weeds, coarser grasses and herbs; unfortunately this also means the depletion of essential medicinal herbs, vitamins and trace minerals. The most useful remedies often come from the untouched green fields and woods all around us. Man's neglect and ignorance of medicinal plants is one of the basic reasons why both human and animal diseases are so widespread; the greatest benefit of using herbal medicines is that because they are natural they can be fully absorbed, whereas synthetic supplements 'clog the system' rather than enhance efficiency. This ultimately hinders the horse's well-being. A few of the most commonly used herbs for horses are outlined below, with a brief indication of their uses: arnica, comfrey, dandelion, garlic, nettle (common) and mint.

Arnica A jar of arnica cream or tincture is a must for any herbal medicine chest; otherwise the entire plant can be used but especially the flower heads. It is for external use only. **Helpful uses:** against bruises, joint stiffness, wounds, swelling, and shock paralysis.

Comfrey This herb is well known for its peculiar powers upon the bones and ligaments: it has the power of aiding the body in the speedy and firm uniting of fractured surfaces, more commonly known as 'knit-bone'. Its name is derived from the Greek work 'to unite'. Both the leaves and roots have medicinal properties. **Helpful uses:** to cure all internal haemorrhages, aid the reunion of wounds, and help knit together fractured and broken bones (especially valued in limb fractures); a valuable remedy for pulmonary ailments; also a proven and effective remedy

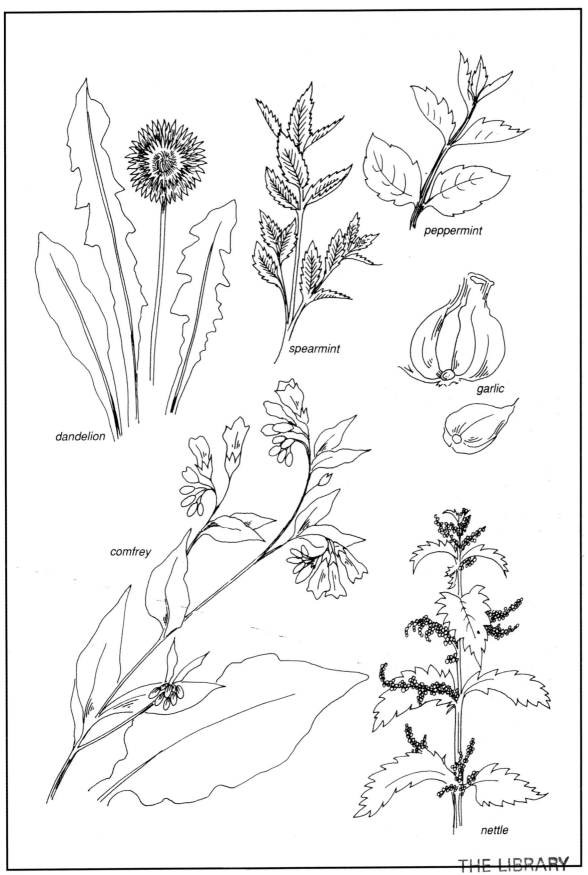

peppermint

spearmint

garlic

dandelion

comfrey

nettle

for rheumatism and arthritis; externally the leaves or roots make a useful poultice for all types of swelling.

Dandelion To the gardener a troublesome weed, yet one of the most valuable known to the herbalist. The dandelion is blood-cleansing and a tonic. It has an important effect upon the hepatic (liver) system. The leaves strengthen the enamel of the teeth; the white juice dissolves warts; it is also a natural diuretic. **Helpful uses:** in the treatment of skin eruptions, sluggish blood flow, weak arteries, all liver and kidney complaints, jaundice and constipation.

Garlic Garlic's outstanding health properties have been appreciated for centuries. Science confirms that many of these benefits do complement the body's natural systems. It is one of the most widely used plants throughout the world, both for medicinal and culinary purposes. Notably, garlic increases resistance to infection; it is also a wonderful preventative measure against minor ailments. **Helpful uses:** antiseptic bactericidal; blood cleanser; decongestant and detoxifier; relieves respiratory and circulation complaints.

Mint (peppermint and spearmint) Mint is highly regarded for its digestive properties, having a beneficial action on the stomach, liver and intestines. This is primarily due to its antispasmodic action which relaxes the smooth muscles of the stomach and gut. **Helpful uses:** against colic, all internal aches and pains; indigestion, also aids the digestive processes; acts as an aphrodisiac for stallions!

Nettle (common) The dried herb is an excellent forage for horses, being very rich in such minerals as iron, lime, sodium and chlorine as well as containing protein. Nettle is an excellent blood detoxifier. Its juices encourage beautiful dappling on horses. **Helpful uses:** entices poor appetite; to counteract heart diseases; lung disorders; blood impurities and disorders (ie anaemia); and worms.

Herbs can provide remarkable cures yet they must always be carefully applied – proper doses and preparation are essential for safe use. Natural diet and herbal treatments work together to ward off disease and cure troublesome ailments – the attainment of perfect equine health should be the key objective! The above examples provide a starting-point for the herb enthusiast, and there are many other sources available to improve herbal knowledge and confirm the power of herbs; but if you need further information it is best to consult an equine herbalist or company specialising in this area.

Stable Management

For the horse to be fit and healthy it is important that it lives in a suitable environment. If stabled, the loosebox should be big enough to allow free movement: ten by twelve feet is considered the minimum size for a horse, and ten by ten feet for ponies that are stabled permanently. Adequate ventilation but without draughts is important, and there should be plenty of light.

Safety at all times is essential: there should be no visible electric wires, either inside or within reach of the horse, and no rough edges or sharp areas which might hurt him.

Clipping

Clipping helps to prevent weight loss, and keeps the horse in good condition once he starts growing his winter coat in the autumn, because it allows you to work him hard without the risk of him getting too hot; with a full winter coat it would be difficult to dry him off properly so he might be liable to chills. Clipping also helps in keeping him clean.

There are various types of clip, and which you choose will depend on your animal's coat and how much work you intend doing with him. The full clip is for the horse in serious work; the hunter clip is ideal for hunters and competition horses who might benefit from the extra protection on their legs, or for those who feel the cold; and the trace and blanket clips are for horses and

• *There are various methods of clipping out the horse according to the type of work he is to do. The blanket clip is very useful for horses doing lighter work or slow work in cold weather*

• *This horse has a variation of the trace clip with just his lower belly off and a narrow strip up the neck. Depending on the work and how hot the horse gets you can adapt the clip to suit your needs*

• *The trace clip with the legs and upper body left unclipped but the head, lower neck and body clipped out*

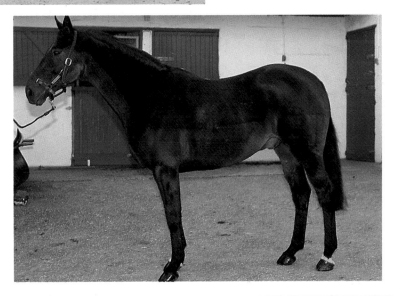

• The traditional hunter clip with legs and saddle patch left on and the rest of the body off

ponies in medium work, or for those ridden at weekends only.

Once the horse's coat gets thick he will start to sweat unduly when worked, and then it is best to clip him as soon as possible to prevent weight loss. During the autumn and winter months, the horse will need to be reclipped every three to six weeks depending how quickly the hair grows. Some horses grow a long, thick coat at other times of the year too, and it is always best to clip these if they get hot, even in the summer months. In the winter I generally do a high trace clip whilst the horses do their slow work, and then a hunter clip when they start to work more seriously.

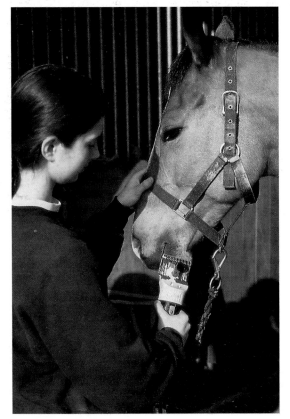

• Trimming whiskers can be done with scissors or clippers if your horse is quiet

1

2

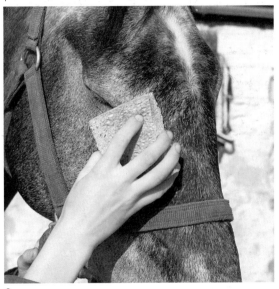

3

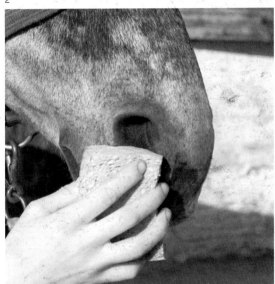

4

● **1** *Regular grooming helps to keep the coat in good condition and the horse clean. It also acts as a good fittening exercise for the rider*

● **2** *Pick straw out of the tail by hand, and use a soft brush to brush the end*

● **3 & 4** *Sponging eyes and nose as well as the dock area is refreshing for the horse*

Grooming

Grooming not only keeps the horse looking and feeling clean, it also acts as a skin massage and helps in the general toning-up process. If your horse is lacking muscle tone or is short of muscle, strapping may help. This is a method whereby the muscles along the neck and quarters are caused to contract and relax by 'banging' them in a slow, steady rhythm with a wisp, soft brush or rolled-up stable rubber. Although in this labour-saving age this extra period of the grooming routine does not happen very often, it is nonetheless beneficial for many horses if done gradually, working up to approximately fifty 'bangs' on either side of the neck and quarters.

● *The hooves must be picked out daily, and before and after riding, to keep them in good condition. This hoof pick has a brush on the end for brushing out the foot. The shoe is worn; check that your horse is regularly shod*

● *Hoof care will ensure the horn stays in good condition. If the horn is dry, oil regularly to help to improve brittle hooves*

Be particularly vigilant over hoof care, and pick the feet out twice a day; attend to any loose clenches, and notice the condition of the feet and legs and of the horse in general so that if there is anything of even slight concern, it gets treated immediately before it becomes a problem.

Shoeing

Shoes will become essential if the working horse is to remain sound, and able to work on the roads or hard ground. However, ponies in particular, and some horses with very hard feet, may be all right without shoes, depending upon the work they will be expected to do – if you are lucky enough to

have an animal which does not require shoes, this will certainly save on costs!

Regular trimming of the feet is vital, to keep them in the right shape and at the right angle, and should be done every four to six weeks, even when the horse is out at grass on holiday. When the horse first comes in or starts to get fit, make sure his feet are in good shape. It is very unwise to start any training or fitness work with feet that are too long, or with shoes that are half on or have been left on but not attended to whilst the horse has had his rest. Working him when his feet are in this state may lead to bruising and corns, and this is certainly not the build-up one wants.

The shoes should be made to fit the horse and its way of going. Ask your farrier to watch your horse trot up so that if it does not move too well or tends to knock itself, he can make any helpful adjustments either to the shoe or the way it is set onto the hoof. These might include feather-edging, or bevelling, where the shape and width is reduced; the use of three-quarter shoes; or for horses that have sensitive feet, wide-webbed shoes that

● *Regular shoeing and foot care is vital to your horse's soundness. Here the farrier is paring the foot before putting on a new set*

increase the weight-bearing surface and so may improve their way of going.

Remember to ask for stud holes if you need extra grip, for example when competing or starting jump-schooling sessions. Always discuss any foot problems with your farrier – he is the expert and can guide you on how to cope with any specific problems relating to your horse's feet.

Exercise

Exercise is vital to every horse's state of health and must be a priority. Food and exercise go together and how much exercise or work your horse has will influence his food intake, especially in stabled horses.

There is a big difference between exercise and work. All horses must have exercise, but not all will necessarily be expected to *work* to any great degree unless specifically asked to do so. Turning a horse out to graze or going out for a gentle hack will count as exercise, but half-an-hour or more practising circles and turns for your dressage test will definitely count as work. Grid-work or fitness training up hills is strenuous. It is most important that the preparation for such work is gradual and not overdone.

Lungeing is another good means of exercise: if a horse is likely to gallop about wildly when let loose in a field it might be wiser and safer to lunge it so that the risk of injury is reduced. Riding one horse and leading another without a rider is a convenient method of exercising two horses if you are short of time. Try and alternate between the one you ride and the one you lead, as the ridden horse may bend more towards the led one, which could lead to one-sidedness.

Always remember to cut down on food if a horse does not go out for exercise at any stage. He can have hay ad lib, but cut out the concentrates and give a bran mash. *Never* feel sorry for him and make it up to him by giving him a nice big supper instead, which is the classic way of causing real problems – he will tend to have filled, swollen legs in the morning anyway, caused by lack of circulation to disperse fluid, and will very probably develop azoturia if then worked hard the next day.

● *If it is not possible to ride or turn the horse out for any reason he can be led out for exercise, especially the day after an outing. Let him eat some grass as often as possible*

● *Riding and leading is a useful way of exercising horses, especially if time is short. If you have to do this regularly alternate the horses to keep back and girth areas hardened on both. Keep the led horse on the inside when on the roads*

Azoturia

This is thought to be caused by too much work following a period of rest, and is typically manifested as a severe and painful seizing-up of the muscles in the hindquarters and back. The horse will slow down and become reluctant to move, showing signs of severe distress and pain. Get off him immediately, and loosen his girths, and do not force him to move as any further exertion will cause further muscle damage. Try to arrange transport home if far away; keep him warm and as still as possible. If the attack is mild it may eventually wear off, when he will seem more willing to move – but this must be of his own accord. If the attack has been bad, the horse's urine will show as dark coffee colour. Azoturia is also known as setfast, Monday morning disease, or blackwater; it tends to affect mares in particular, and is prevalent in the heavier types of animal as well as those in strenuous work as already discussed.

In a bad case, call the vet immediately. He will treat the horse with muscle relaxants and painkillers, and will usually take a blood sample to assess the degree of muscle damage; this will determine how soon the horse will be able to return to work – this may be in a few days, in a serious case it may be weeks. Whichever it is, the same principle applies: increase the work slowly, building up day by day. Talk to your vet about future work, and whether your feeding routine requires modification.

Fitness Training for the Horse

When starting all fitness work remember the basic principles: first, make haste slowly and do not do too much, too soon. Build up the horse's work gradually, and assess his physical state regularly before you increase it. Traditionally in Britain horses have always started their fitness work on the roads in walk, the theory being that the smooth level surface removes the risk of strain or tripping which might otherwise be incurred by riding on an uneven surface with muscles and tendons that are soft and out of condition.

For centuries this has proved itself the

ideal start to the fitness programme. Stud grooms kept a watchful eye on the horse's progress, and the trot work which followed the walking phase was kept very slow so the muscles had time to extend and contract, and the tendons tightened and were toned to be in peak condition before any serious work started. This period usually took up to eight to twelve weeks, and the horse was then ready for anything. I would not go so far as to say that they had no problems, but it does apear that modern techniques tend to hurry that all-important basic phase of hardening and toning the legs – and of course, other muscles – in readiness for the more strenuous work to come.

While there are more horses competing now than ever before there does also appear to be a dramatic rise in fitness-related problems. I have spoken to several vets on the subject and their assessment appears to be this:

1 Too much is expected too soon.
2 Horses are asked to do too much when they are too young, and this does affect them later on.
3 Not enough attention is paid to foot care, and the fact that any imbalance will ultimately affect the horse's way of going and his muscular development.
4 Many riders do not recognise the differ

● *Fitness work starts with slow work, but once that stage is over longer hacks out can be undertaken. Riding in a group is good for the horse so that he gets used to others as well as working alone*

ence between a fit horse, and a half-fit horse which should not be expected to do many of the things asked of it in this competitive world.

Fitness training for the horse can be divided into three main stages: first, slow work; second the build-up to whatever it is you have set your sights on; and finally the fine tuning required to compete.

Training Phase One

Slow work This starts at walk, ideally on the road commencing at a natural pace with the horse held lightly between hand and leg. He should not be expected to hold himself up together for too long for the first week, although he should be kept reasonably balanced and purposeful to ensure he doesn't trip or stumble in his unfit state.

If the horse was having no hard feed before he came in, twenty to thirty minutes would probably be enough for the first few days; if he has, then thirty to forty-five minutes walking should not worry him. By the end of the first week he should be doing forty-five minutes to one hour's walking.

I believe implicitly that it is worth spending time at this slow stage, having found through experience that the longer you spend walking – particularly if you can include hills in your routes – the better the horses cope with the second and third stages.

The second week will be spent increasing the work a little, to begin with walking for forty-five minutes to one hour, until you have extended the exercise to one-and-a-half hours. During this time the horse must be asked to use himself more, and should be pushed into a rounded outline, walking forwards well on to the bit. Remember to give

periods of relaxation, but never allow the horse to slop along on a loose rein; always have him in balance.

Depending on what your horse is ultimately aiming for, and having done the first two weeks in walk, you should now decide whether to continue in walk or to commence the walk-and-trot stage. In general, horses not expected to do anything too strenuous (such as galloping or jumping) will probably be quite safe from the risk of strain or injury in the long term if they started steady trotting in the third week. Start as usual at walk for about half-an-hour, and then do periods of steady trotting. Keep this as slow as possible, but ask your horse to remain on the bit and push him up into his bridle with your legs. Progress gradually by doing a little more trotting, or trot for longer in between periods of walk.

For horses aiming for more serious ultimate work, it is as well to continue in walk for another one to two weeks. Furthermore if the horse has ever had any tendon problem he should certainly have this time in walk, and for serious cases walking should continue for anything from six to twelve weeks before slow trotting is gradually included.

Hills If you have hills nearby that are not so steep as to risk causing strain, then working up and down these is perfect for building up fitness. Remember to keep the horse together, but allow enough rein so he can stretch forwards and go up the hills with ease. You should change diagonals frequently, especially when going uphill, to ensure even muscle development on each side. Not doing so is one of the classic reasons for back and hock problems, and many people do not realise the harm they do by remaining on one diagonal when working a horse. In most cases when you change diagonal it is easy to feel the difference between the horse's good side and its stiffer one.

Be careful not to overdo hillwork in the early stages, and avoid hills altogether for the first two weeks, only introducing them gradually from then onwards. It would be ideal if you can work out some good rides that include hillwork three times a week.

● *The horse must be made to work on the bit to build up muscle and fitness. This horse is a little overbent, with his nose back behind the vertical, but he is going forward well. The rider is practising without stirrups and has a good seat and leg position*

Varying the work Being on the roads in these first few weeks need not mean that walking or walking and trotting is necessarily boring. This slow stage when muscle is being built up, and tendons and ligaments toned, is perhaps one of the most important stages in your build-up programme and provides the ideal chance to improve suppleness. For example, out on a ride you can practise half-halts, a little shoulder-in, neck-bends to the right and left, halting and so on, and it is a wonderful chance to work at establishing a rhythm. Allow your horse a chance to relax and stretch his neck whenever possible so that he does not become tight in his muscles, which is a fault often seen; every period of work must be followed

● *The value of hills cannot be overemphasised. Not only does it make the horse work harder, but going up hills helps to save the strain on a horse's front legs, and is particularly useful for competition horses. It is important to keep the weight forward and in balance when working up hills whether in walk, trot or canter*

by a period of relaxing and stretching. Be careful, however, not to allow the horse to get so relaxed that he trips up or stumbles; some people use skeleton kneecaps when doing road work to prevent injury in such a situation.

Once the horse is doing more strenuous work – trotting for longer periods – the time he is out on exercise can be reduced, an hour and a half being the general rule – though a longer ride once or twice a week is a good idea if your horse is coping with his programme well. However, always remember that you are dealing with an individual, and if he is finding the work tiring then ease up on this for a few days and assess your feeding routine to see if he is having the right quality and quantities of food for the work being done. His shoes will need to be attended to regularly during this period, as he will tend to wear them down in a couple of weeks.

Training Phase Two

Once the initial stage of fitness work is completed, the horse should be sufficiently toned up to commence some serious work for short periods. Always start off by going for a hack so that the circulation is properly stimulated and the horse is settled and relaxed; initially an hour's hack followed by ten minutes in the school or field should suffice. Gradually over the following two weeks less hacking and more school work can be the rule – though I believe the horse needs at least two complete breaks from schooling, one at the weekend which can be a day off, and one midweek when a gentle hack would be relaxing. He can work on the other days doing suppling work in the school.

Suppling exercises Once the horse is properly loosened up he can go in the school where the various exercises help supple him and build up muscle and power. Always start out in the school aiming to achieve something new every day. Your ultimate objective is a supple horse with loose flowing paces, and one which is obedient to the aids. Aim for equal suppleness on each rein, and therefore try to do the same amount of work in both directions. However, inevitably some horses are stiffer on one side than the other, so you may need to work on the stiff side more until the horse loosens. Remember it is always a mistake to rush things, as this tends to create tension and even greater stiffness.

Circles Working on circles constitutes the best basic exercise you can use to loosen and create suppleness in the horse, and should be included early in the horse's training. The horse should be bent evenly round the rider's inside leg, his body following the shape of the circle; performed correctly, the inside hind leg has to work a little harder, as do the muscles along the rib cage – on the outside these have to assume a longer shape, so there is stretching on the outside of the horse and shortening along the inside.

Start with large circles, maintaining an even rhythm, but keep varying the direction and size – 20m and on occasions down to 10m should make the horse more supple. As fitness increases the horse can be asked to do a 20m circle or circles at different spots round the school, for example at A, E, C or B. More advanced horses can do smaller circles – though remember, the smaller the circle the more strenuous it is, and unless the horse is balanced and in self-carriage (holding himself between the rider's hand and leg) he will not be using himself correctly and so will not be working properly and building up the correct muscle.

Serpentines This is another excellent suppling exercise requiring changes of direction and bend whilst maintaining rhythm and balance throughout. Generally in a 20 × 40m school it is usual to do three loops, but if you are outside or in a bigger arena you can do as many as you can fit into the area available. The main concern in this exercise is to maintain an even forward rhythm and to change the bend over the centre line when you prepare to go in the opposite direction. Once you have mastered the three loops, try to fit in another one or two by making the loops more acute by accentuating the bend.

There are numerous variations to the above two exercises, such as loops and half circles, all requiring the same essentials of rhythm and balance and change of direction. One of the main faults to be seen when riders perform these movements is that they tend to forget the first basic principle of riding, which is the importance of free forward movement. No exercise of any sort will be of any benefit whatsoever if the horse is not going confidently forwards into the bridle.

SERPENTINES, CIRCLES AND LOOPS

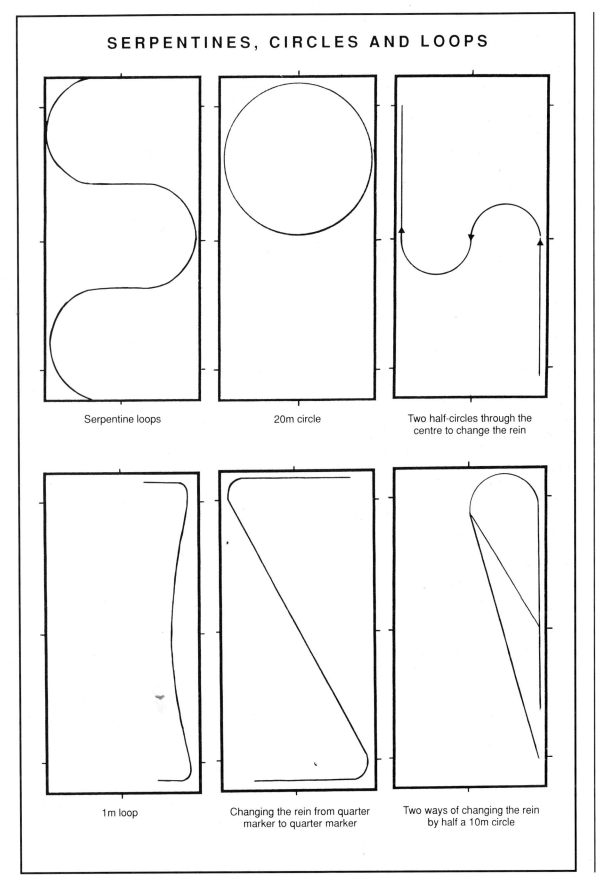

Serpentine loops

20m circle

Two half-circles through the
centre to change the rein

1m loop

Changing the rein from quarter
marker to quarter marker

Two ways of changing the rein
by half a 10m circle

● Pole work is invaluable when schooling horses as it helps to improve balance and co-ordination and makes jumping so much easier afterwards. This horse is really using itself over these special raised poles and stepping centrally through them. Make sure the poles are set at the right distance for the horse's stride

Pole work This is an excellent way to supple the horse and add variation to his work: because he actually has to step over the poles he is made to work that little bit harder than when working normally in the arena. There are numerous exercises which can be used, but until your horse is used to poles, keep things simple or he will tense up in anticipation and the whole purpose of the exercise will be lost – that is, that he is relaxed in his work over poles to increase suppleness.

If you are on your own, the best method is to place four to six poles (more if you have them) in a row 3m (9 to 10ft) apart; the horse will be able to put one complete stride in between the poles. This allows for versatility, and means you will not have to get off to change anything unless a pole gets knocked seriously out of position. If you have a helper you can start them closer together so that you use them at trotting distance of 1.5m (4ft 6in) approximately.

Start by trotting over them quietly, making sure the horse is relaxed and settled into a good rhythm. Once this has been achieved you can vary the exercise and try trotting through the poles as a serpentine, bending round every second pole. Eventually you will be able to bend round every pole as your horse loosens sufficiently and relaxes. The secret is not to rush any of the exercise so that the horse adjusts his own balance and rhythm.

The diagrams show some of the variations in the exercises that can be performed over and through the poles. A nervous horse who perhaps becomes very tense on the flat may be much more relaxed once he has settled over poles – they seem to take the horse's mind off himself as he has to concentrate that much more to cope with the changes of direction and the lift required to trot over the poles. If the horse is working correctly you will be amazed at the improvement in his rhythm once he settles to his work. Pole work is also helpful to the rider as it develops co-ordination and balance as well as mental awareness. Finally, it is an excellent introduction to jumping.

POLEWORK

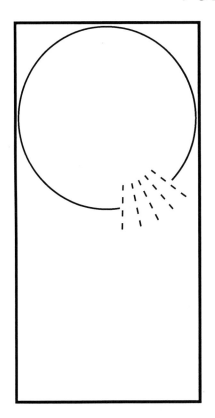

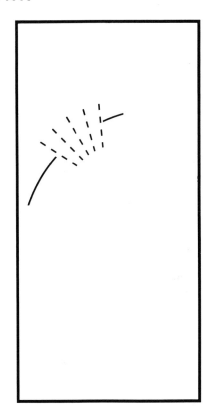

Working over poles is an excellent way to supple the horse. Stepping over the poles makes him work harder than normal arena work.

The poles, which should be placed at trotting distance (1.5m) apart, can be

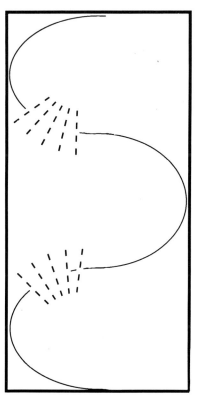

placed on the straight, on a 20m circle, on a curve or on the serpentine.

Raising the poles will encourage more engagement of the hind legs, giving more elevated steps

Transitions Variations within a pace and from one pace to another will help towards mental alertness and lightness in front. With all work it is most important to change and vary what you are doing, so that the horse remains responsive and attentive to the rider's wishes. So often you see riders going round and round, doing the same thing over and over again with no emphasis on any one aspect. Like any other animal or even human, the horse will only progress if it is pushed a little and given some incentive – so be positive about when and where you want a transition to happen, and really work on making a difference between a working to a medium or extended movement, and prepare the horse well with a half-halt before changing from one pace to another.

Lateral work For anyone attempting lateral work for the first time it is best to start with leg-yielding: this entails pushing the horse sideways and forwards, but with the head almost straight or slightly away from the direction in which he should be going. In essence the horse is responding to the leg-aid in its simplest form.

One of the most effective suppling exercises is the shoulder-in, as it demands a high degree of bend and sideways movement away from the direction in which you are travelling. The horse is therefore having to increase the use of his joints, particularly those of the hip, stifle and hock on the inside. He is required to move freely forwards, but this is made more demanding by the bend through the back and shoulder; thus it is important for the rider to allow enough freedom yet ask for impulsion throughout.

The most advanced form of lateral work is the half-pass, in which the horse moves forwards and sideways whilst maintaining the bend towards the direction in which he is travelling; greater flexion and more energy is required to perform this movement. If you are relatively inexperienced it is best to learn leg-yielding and shoulder-in before embarking on half-pass, which does require a certain knowledge and expertise if you are not to risk doing it incorrectly. Having a trainer who knows what is required will save you this problem!

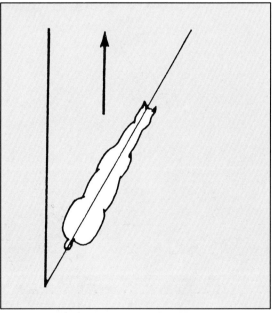

● *Leg-yielding is a useful exercise to accustom the horse to more advanced lateral work. It is simply a method of asking the horse to go away from the rider's leg, and is usually done in walk or trot. The head does not look in the direction that the horse is going*

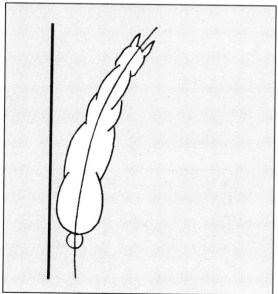

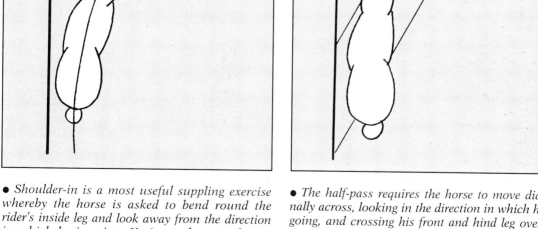

● Shoulder-in is a most useful suppling exercise whereby the horse is asked to bend round the rider's inside leg and look away from the direction in which he is going. He is on three tracks. As progress is made the degree of angle can be increased so that there is even more bend through the body

● The half-pass requires the horse to move diagonally across, looking in the direction in which he is going, and crossing his front and hind leg over in front of the opposite ones. It is a progression from the shoulder-in and requires a certain amount of collection and balance to be successful

Counter canter This is another excellent exercise designed to loosen and supple the horse, though he may find it a bit difficult at first if you try it in too confined a space. Give yourself plenty of room to start with, and keep the contact on the leading side so that there is no danger of the horse wanting to change legs. As you change direction, the canter lead ends up on the outside and it is important that you **keep your weight towards this leading leg at all times**. Counter canter is in fact a balanced canter on the wrong leg, and it is the shift in your weight that will influence the horse's balance and make him change.

Counter canter is useful as a suppling exercise as it increases the ability of the horse to balance and support itself. A horse on its forehand will find this exercise very difficult, whereas a naturally well-balanced one will not, even if it is not really 'up together' and between hand and leg.

Gymnastic jumping For the horse and rider who want to jump, gridwork is the ideal way for any jumper both to start and to build up to peak fitness. While different sports demand different types of jumping, grids will teach any horse to be alert and athletic and will help to develop his jumping ability. Always start with a couple of simple fences to allow the horse to realise what is required, then build up the grid gradually – suddenly confronting him with a mass of poles is the best way to undermine his confidence! If you have included pole work in your training the horse should already be relaxed about this sort of exercise, so grids should present few problems.

A cross pole encourages the horse to stay in the middle of the fence, and because of the high sides it also helps the horse to jump higher in front and so encourages a round jump. A straight fence demands accuracy, and parallels or wider fences require the horse to bascule and jump bigger to clear both width and height; thus if you incorporate a combination of these in your grid you are helping the horse to master several exercises at once. All this teaches him to think and balance himself whilst using all his muscles to negotiate the fences involved; it also helps him to develop a correct technique.

Bigger fences are not particularly important until you reach a certain standard, when size plays a major part – such as in open show jumping. For the average 3ft 6in course and most riding club or Pony Club activities, it will not be necessary to aim higher unless you want to progress further.

Never overdo gymnastic jumping; once or twice a week will be plenty, as the horse has to work quite hard in a short period of time – and always stop when things are going well. If you have a problem going through a grid, lower the fences or make the exercise easier, then build up again gradually. You

may have asked too much, so be ready to ease off if you feel the horse has made a mistake and lost confidence. If it is *you* then consider what mistake you might have made, and try to remedy it there and then.

If it is impossible to organise a grid session, practise over a couple of single fences, an upright and a spread, and see if you can jump successfully off both reins. Try to find a good line off a corner, or turn into the school so as to jump your fence off a turn. All this will help with balance and motivation, quite apart from increasing general fitness.

Personally, I believe all horses should be

● *Gymnastic jumping helps to improve the horse's jumping technique. The rider is allowing the horse complete freedom to use itself properly over this fence at the end of the grid. The horse is lowering its head and 'rounding' well over the obstacle*

able to jump, even if this is not to be a part of their future plans – a little jumping is good for everyone as it improves balance and confidence, and will ensure that you are both prepared for any eventuality, even when out hacking: if ever you have to leave the ground the horse will know what to do, and so will you.

Assessment of phase two Any of the above exercises used in conjunction with daily hacks should build up your horse's fitness enough for him to be able to cope with most activities in moderation after four to six weeks' work. For those aiming higher the horse will need more fitness training, depending upon the nature of the work you want him to do. Generally if you can hack out two or three times a week, and work him on the flat or over fences two or three times a week once his basic fitness is complete, the horse would be ready for most riding club or Pony Club activities, or general everyday riding.

The best guide as to whether he is getting the right amount of feed and work is if he looks and feels well. If he is losing too much weight or feels dull and listless then probably you should increase the feed, also check you have kept up to date with worming, and reassess your work programme. A few days off in the field may also help. Like us, horses can get a bit bored or demoralised, so a short break may make an enormous difference.

For the needs of most people the horse will probably be fit enough by now; however, for those aiming for more strenuous work – competing in hunter trials, horse trials or show jumping – there is a third phase of training which involves final preparatory work for the chosen sport. This might be fast work for such as event horses or point-to-pointers, more specific jumping practice for show jumpers, or riding tests for dressage riders (for further details, see Chapter 5).

Training Phase Three

Canter work Cantering helps to build up the endurance ability of the horse; like the slower paces, to start with it should be steady or over a relatively short distance. This will gradually be increased so that a strong, steady canter is performed twice a week. Many horses sound a bit thick in their wind to start with, but after two or three canters this generally improves.

Always choose good ground for your canter work, and make sure you have adequate brakes! – a galloping horse out of control is liable to damage itself, and if cantering with a large expanse of grass stretching out in front, it may well take off if you are not prepared.

Galloping It is rarely necessary to gallop a horse in the proper sense of the word, unless it is in training for racing, point-to-pointing or three-day eventing when such work is important to the final stages of fitness. Long, steady cantering which has started slowly and been built up gradually is the ideal, and if this progresses into stronger work, with the odd gallop over half to three-quarters of a mile at the end, the horse will be increasing his capacity for fast work.

To improve his stamina the horse needs to work fast so that he *does* get into the anaerobic state: this will be important when he is in training for endurance work such as the three-day event. This is because muscles can adapt to the demands made in training, in so far as some muscle fibres are able to use more oxygen than others; obviously the more there are of these and the more demands placed on them in similar circumstances to those that would be met when competing, the better able they will be to cope with the work. The horse will therefore be able to work harder and faster before the build-up of lactic acid begins. (Further galloping work will be discussed in the relevant sections.)

Injuries in training: Inevitably the more work the horse does, the more chance there is of injury. Fast work in particular increases the risk, especially if the horse is not really fit enough or has been ridden beyond his level of fitness.

Strained tendons are probably the most common injury in horses doing fast work. It is therefore very important to watch out for any signs of heat or pain around the tendons, and to treat the slightest sign of a problem with caution.

Joints, and particularly the fetlock, are especially vulnerable in the jumping horse, and any signs of strain or jarring should be treated systematically. Always remember the effect hard ground can have on a horse and only ride when absolutely necessary over big courses in such conditions.

Feet are inevitably prone to bruising and jarring, and for this reason should be

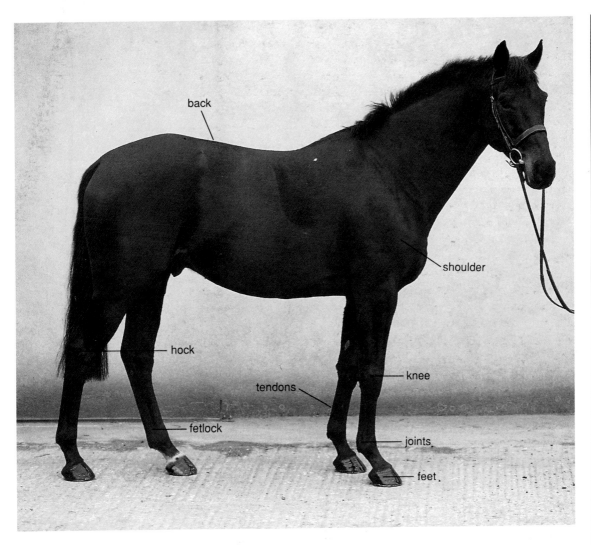

back

shoulder

hock

tendons

knee

fetlock

joints

feet

checked regularly and never allowed to grow too long, this is especially true of the toe, as it would put added strain on the back of the tendons.

The horse's back has to put up with all manner of situations with the human weight on top of it, and any sudden, awkward movements such as a slip, a fall, or a cold draught on the long muscles could cause a problem here. There are specialists who treat backs successfully, who can manipulate muscles and relieve tightness should this be felt to be a problem.

Cuts and bruises can happen at any time but should always be treated by careful cleaning and an appropriate dressing. Overreaches are particularly common.

Signs of fitness The fit horse is difficult to assess, but it should look like a healthy horse

● *The competition horse in particular is prone to injury, but these can be minimised by a correct and careful build-up in fitness. Strains are probably the most common injuries to tendons, back, shoulders and occasionally hocks. Jarring to the joints on hard ground, and injuries to the foot through bruising or bad shoeing, are other common problems. Knees and fetlocks are liable to knocks in the jumping horse particularly if the rider tends to be in the wrong position or is riding too fast*

in every way – that is, alert and cheerful, with glossy coat and bright eye. The body should look tight and have a slightly drawn up appearance when the horse is beginning to get really fit. You may be able to feel ribs at this stage but the horse should still have plenty of muscle over his back and loins. His legs should look tough and hard with well-defined tendons. He should give the appearance of a horse in the peak of condition.

4 ADVANCED MANAGEMENT & TRAINING

As with anything in life, there are limits to what can be achieved, and these depend largely on individual circumstances. The latter may affect the rider or the horse or both, and full satisfaction can only be obtained if a realistic goal is set in the first place. The two most important considerations have to be time and expense. Look carefully at both of these, and if you feel you can cope then it is up to you to have the necessary commitment to be able to carry out your aims.

Costs, Care and Management

Look at the type of horse you have and consider carefully whether he would be capable, if carefully trained and produced, to do what you have in mind. Remember that not every horse, however perfect, will feel the necessary inclination to be a show jumper, or a dressage horse, or whatever it is that you want it to be, so you may have to make the difficult decision of selling it on and getting something more suitable. The other alternative is to keep the horse, but adapt your ideas to fit more closely with what he might actually do quite well. He might be good at dressage, having nice paces; maybe his conformation is such that he would excel in the show ring.

A Thoroughbred horse might be a good point-to-pointer, polo pony, eventer or even a dressage horse if he has a calm temperament. The warmblood is renowned for its jumping ability and movement; the native ponies are excellent children's mounts, with the Welsh and Connemara excelling at the all-round sports and activities practised widely in the Pony Club. All manner of sports can be enjoyed by so many people in different ways, whether the horse or pony lives out all year round, is kept partially stabled, or is kept in all the time.

Obviously at the higher levels of any sport you will need to have the right facilities available, but it is amazing how well people cope if they have the determination to succeed. As you get to know more people in a sport you will realise how many others are just as mad about it as yourself – and one thing leads to another . . . However, you must always be realistic: talk to others, so you really do understand what is involved, and look into all the anticipated running costs of your horse, and what you will need for your sport and your future progress. Your decision as to whether to continue or not, is then usually only a formality.

Nonetheless horses are a tie, and they do take up a lot of time; nor can you just lock the door on them and go away for a few days. They need feeding, shoeing and veterinary care; they also need a paddock and/or stable and all the maintenance involved with that. They will need rugs, tack, and leg protection in the form of boots or bandages. You should also have a stock of simple first-aid remedies and poultices, fly sprays, mucking-out tools, buckets, feed mangers, haynets. I am afraid the list is endless, but it must be thought about before you embark on doing anything seriously because, of course, it constitutes a part of the financial side.

The Grass-kept Horse

The ideal is to own a paddock, but a horse will need at least one to three acres of grazing if he is to stay out all the time. Moreover careful paddock management is essential, especially with only a small acreage. However, grazing is the most natural and economical method, provided that you have good fencing, access to fresh water and your field is safe from sharp objects, poisonous plants, rabbit holes and so on, and that there is shelter.

Paddock Management

Good management of the grazing area is most important, especially if it is limited. How you cope very much depends on how much land you have and whether you can alternate grazing for your horse or not. All small paddocks require droppings to be picked up regularly – daily, if possible – to keep the land clear from worm infestation. If you share paddocks with others, get together over your worming routine and ensure that *all* horses are done at the same time. At some stage the land will need a rest, and all horses should come off together and go elsewhere. If this is not possible, strip grazing can be quite successful: move the animals to a different area or field whilst the other is harrowed and rested – ideally it should be grazed by cattle, as these will eat down the coarser grasses which horses leave. If sheep are stocked afterwards they will eat the grass and weeds right down and leave the land clear and ready for a fresh, even growth. Ideally a pasture should be rested for at least three months a year if it is not to become gradually horse-sick.

Paddocks will also require fertilising regularly, especially if a soil analysis shows them to be deficient in any way; the application of nitrogen, potash, phosphate, lime, or whatever is relevant, should put this right. An annual soil analysis may be beneficial anyway, especially if your horse is not doing too well in spite of your efforts with supplementary feeding.

Weeds have a horrid habit of cropping up when least wanted. Since the introduction of 'set-aside', many of these have increased in alarming proportions, especially ragwort which is known to be particularly harmful to horses if eaten when it is in its wilting state. Although it is not often that horses will touch this, certainly if there is plenty of grazing available, they may well resort to it if the grass is poor or sparse; and the ingestion of ragwort can result in a slow deterioration of the liver. If this plant with its distinctive yellow flower appears in your paddock it should

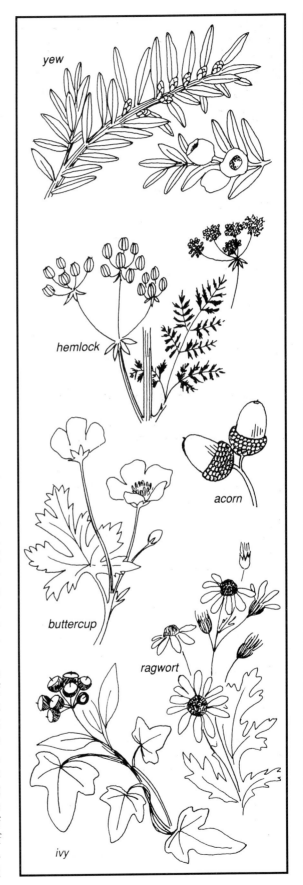

be pulled up, root and all, *before* it goes to seed. Spraying the young growth by hand may help to prevent future spread, but the horse must be kept out of the field for some time to ensure it will not be tempted to eat any of it in its wilting state. Hemlock, yew, buttercups, ivy and acorns are all dangerous to the horse, which must be kept away from them if accidents are not to happen.

Harrowing and rolling will help to keep the land in good condition. Harrowing scratches the loose dead grass around and aerates the ground, as well as spreading the droppings from the areas which the horse, as a selective eater, will not graze. Rolling will flatten the soil and iron out hoof marks and cut-up ground which would otherwise become very rough and rutted in dry weather. If you cannot do this yourself, a friendly neighbour may do it for you if he has the equipment. However, sometimes you have to improvise, and drag around some form of wire mesh and a weight or even a large garden rake! Nevertheless, your land will definitely benefit from being harrowed, however it is accomplished.

Nettles and docks will need to be cut with a hook or a strimmer as they will prevent the grass growing; if they are bad, spraying may be recommended, as long as you can remove the horses.

In general, pastureland needs a good going over in the spring and again in the autumn. At the same time, check fencing, gates and watering facilities carefully, so that all is in good order for the summer and winter.

Fencing

Well-maintained hedges and walls are often the best but are hard to find nowadays, and those in use may well need extra posts and rails added to weak spots. Hedges should be kept trimmed, but should be allowed to grow high enough to give some protection from the elements, especially if there is no other form of shelter.

Post and rails are ideal if the fencing is well constructed and solid. Keep a daily check in case a rail gets broken or your horse manages to squeeze through any possible gap. Always attend to repairs immediately to prevent accidents, and be sure there are no protruding nails which could cause injury.

Whilst wire fencing is not ideal, it is effective so long as the wire is kept taut at all times. It is safer with a rail along the top which can be seen more easily. Barbed wire should never be used near horses – it is potentially extremely dangerous, and horrific injuries have been caused to horses that have become tangled up in it.

● *Barbed wire is not good for horses; it is difficult to see and can cause horrific cuts and tears should a horse become entangled. If it must be used it is vital that it is kept taut and preferably electrified; horses soon learn to respect such fences*

There are numerous 'new' types of fencing on the market which combine a mixture of wire and plastic; many of these may be excellent, but it is worth talking to someone who has actually used these as all too often the initially smart, tight fence has become an untidy sagging line a couple of years later. Be sure you understand the maintenance involved.

Horses are notorious for chewing fences and trees, and it is your responsibility to try to keep this to a minimum, not only to prevent fences being weakened and trees damaged, but to try to keep your place looking tidy and well managed. Creosote should be

● ABOVE: *A well-maintained hedge and rails with wire mesh making an excellent fence through which no horse should be able to escape!*

● RIGHT: *The ideal fencing for horses. A well-constructed post-and-rail fence with good shelter to protect the animals from the prevailing winds*

● BELOW: *Another fairly effective fence, with the dangerous barbed wire protected by a good top rail. So long as the wire and wire mesh are kept tight it should provide a safe fence*

● BELOW RIGHT: *The slack and untidy appearance of this fence does not make for an attractive picture. However, if properly tightened this electric fencing could be very effective as horses quickly learn to respect the wire once they have had a shock*

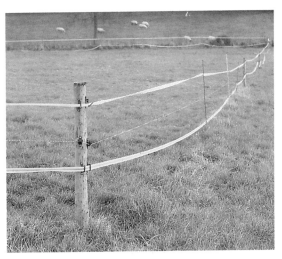

● *Gates with good fastenings are essential. They should be kept locked if they open onto a road or lead into the open*

used regularly on any trees vulnerable to chewing, and all fencing should be done twice a year – remembering gates and gate posts, which are also favourites.

Some people use electric fencing which, put up safely and maintained with batteries, is most effective when laid along the top of the original fencing – horses very quickly learn what it is there for. However, avoid using a very powerful current which may cause them to panic.

Gates must be easy to open and shut so that you can get your horse in and out of the field without a struggle, but they should be kept locked if they open onto a highway or are out of sight, as walkers do unfortunately sometimes leave them open; this is also an added precaution against theft. Make sure the catches are safe, and also horse-proof – with certain fastenings a horse having a rub against a gate can often knock the catch and open it. I always put a chain round my gates as an added precaution, whether or not they are locked.

Shelter and Protective Clothing

Shelter is essential to the horse and must be provided in some form – a couple of good leafy trees, or ideally a three-sided shelter or barn is a must against the wind and rain in winter and the flies in summer. In winter, trees offer little protection unless they are evergreens, but in summer their shade is ideal against the sun. Other buildings adjoining your field may well offer some shelter from strong wind and rain, but if your horse is to be out completely, some further protection is essential. The horse's great friend is, of course, the New Zealand rug, invaluable during the cold winter months; and if it is in good condition and not too heavy, it can be put on whenever the weather is cold or wet at other times of the year.

Made of various types of weather-proof materials and lined with warm fabric, the New Zealand rug is specially shaped and designed with leg straps to keep it in place and prevent it moving when the horse lies down or rolls. It must be the right size for the horse, and the leg straps must be crossed through each other to prevent them chafing the sensitive skin of the horse's inside hind legs. These straps should be kept well oiled and supple if made of leather.

It is a good idea to have two of these rugs if your horse is to live out completely, so that should one get torn or really wet you can change it. The New Zealand was originally made of canvas which was rather heavy; nowadays, modern fabrics have ensured a much lighter rug, but checks should still be made daily to ensure that withers, shoulders and hips are not getting sore or rubbed through the friction of movement. When stabled horses are turned out in the yard or field for exercise during wet or

● *Shelter is important all year round: as protection from flies in summer, and from the cold and wet in winter*

● *The New Zealand rug is a great asset for the horse that is out in the field in all weathers. Make sure the leg straps are crossed to prevent chafing. Pull-on hoods can also be used if it is very cold; some people use them to keep the horse clean as well. They can be very helpful in keeping the mane on the right side*

cold weather New Zealands are used. Some of these rugs also have hood and neck protectors which certainly help to keep the whole horse warm, and above all, clean! If time is one of your problems, this will certainly save hours of brushing!

Water

Water is vital to life and a very important consideration when planning for the grass-kept horse. Fresh water must be permanently available and easily accessible. A running stream or freshwater pond is ideal so long as the horse can drink from these easily. Stagnant water is not good, and if possible should be fenced off.

The most common form of water provision is from a piped, self-filling water trough. Remember to clean this out if it has not been used, as the sitting water will have become stale and stagnant. Make sure the trough is safe with no sharp edges, with the lid over the ballcock kept firmly closed. In winter, troughs tend to freeze up, but it will help if you protect the pipe and side of the ballcock valves by piling straw manure up round the sides or lagging it in some other way. Breaking the ice on a twice-daily basis is most important. When planning the site of a new trough, remember that you may well have to attend to it during the winter so the closer it is to the stables or your own house or water the easier it will be to attend to properly.

For fields with no water laid on at all, you will have to fill a large container daily.

Horses and ponies generally drink between six to twelve gallons a day, and more is consumed in hot weather. Have a large tub or container that will not be knocked over, and refill this twice a day or as necessary.

Feeding the Horse at Grass

What you feed will depend on the type of animal you have, the work it is doing, and how much grazing you have available. Youngsters or horses in hard work will need more good quality grass than horses in their prime ridden just at weekends. The fat pony or horse prone to laminitis (inflammation of the sensitive laminae in the feet) should be kept on very little grass.

If there is plenty of grass, and as long as he looks well and does not get tired doing what is expected of him, your horse may not need much else. This will almost certainly be the case in the spring and early summer when the grass is at its richest and best. However, when there is not much grazing your horse is likely to need extra food to maintain condition, particularly if you are working him. This may take the form of one or two feeds a day; if the horse is not working too hard but is simply short of grass, provide some hay either in a hayrack, on the ground if he does not waste it, or tied up high enough in a haynet which will not drop too low as it empties to risk his putting a foot in it.

In the autumn and winter large mineral feeding blocks are available; these can be put out in the paddock in containers for the horse to lick at random, and will provide all the necessary minerals and trace elements – for many horses this is all they need, along with hay as roughage.

Any extra feeding required should be introduced, gradually, to find out exactly what extra your horse needs. One feed a day of a coarse mix or compound cubes at 9–12 per cent protein should keep your horse in good shape, particularly if he is only being ridden at weekends. However, this will very much depend on your horse's make and shape, his temperament, age, condition, the weather, and how much food there is already in your paddock. As long as a regular worming programme has been maintained – and this is particularly important for the grass-kept horse on a small acreage, which is not easy to maintain in a relatively worm-free state – your horse should be in fairly good condition; but never forget that extra work, getting hot and sweaty, or cold weather which will cause food stores to be used as energy to keep warm – all these will affect the condition of your horse. There is little goodness in the grass from late summer through to early spring, so this is when you will need to add to your horse's diet.

General Care of the Grass-kept Horse

First and foremost is the regular daily check to ensure the horse is well and sound: look at his legs and keep a close eye on his feet, particularly if he is shod – watch the condition of feet and shoes when it is muddy, especially. Personally I do not oil the feet of horses out at grass if it is damp or wet, as moisture is absorbed through their feet and extra oil will only make the hooves softer. In very hard and hot conditions, however, the feet tend to dry out so oiling and/or hoof dressing two or three times a week would then be beneficial. The feet should be picked out every day.

The mane and tail of the grass-kept horse should be kept neat and tidy but not too short. In summer, a longer forelock and tail will be more effective against flies; in winter, a longer mane will be warmer, although the tail could perhaps be kept shorter so that he does not get cold wet hairs around his heels and legs.

The grass-kept horse should not be groomed during the winter except to remove excess mud and dirt, as the oil and grease that builds up in the coat will act as extra warmth against the cold and wet. For this reason also the legs should not be washed, but kept slightly trimmed so that mud does not build up on the long heel hair (feather) which could cause soreness or cracked heels. If there is any sign of soreness in the heels, clean the area and dry carefully before applying a suitable anti-bacterial cream. Applying Vaseline to clean heels may help to prevent recurrence.

● *This horse is blanket clipped, which is useful for the horse that is working but does not need to be clipped out. It keeps the back a little warmer and is ideal for horses coming back into work and those that feel the cold*

Working the Horse from Grass

This routine is quite all right if the horse is kept in good condition and his shoes are in place. Whether you ride daily, or only at weekends, or intermittently does not matter so long as you do not overwork him at any one time. Fast work could cause strain or injury if he is not fit enough, likewise jumping if his basic fitness has not been built up properly.

In the summer the horse will have been wandering about on firm ground for some weeks and this in itself will have hardened and strengthened tendons and muscles, particularly if he is interested in what is going on around him and moves around a lot. The idle horse, on the other hand, will probably not stir himself any more in the field than he does when you ride him. In the winter, with softer ground, the horse's legs will be softer too, and less able to cope with the effort required to get through wet and soggy going; it is at this time that special care must be taken not to overwork your horse.

Your fitness programme can be the same as the one already discussed in Chapter 3 but it may take longer to reach the same level of fitness if you cannot ride regularly or get help to do so. What will be different –

and certainly more awkward – is when you want to do more strenuous work and your horse has been guzzling away up until the time you catch him. As we have already discussed, a horse should not work too hard on a full stomach, and if you plan some serious work your horse should be brought in and given an hour or so without food; if this is difficult, it may be wise to put a muzzle on him for an hour or so before you ride him if you intend to have a gallop or a jumping session. Having said this, horses are remarkably accommodating animals and quickly adapt to their lifestyle; thus they will probably be perfectly all right if *as a rule* they do not eat too much – but for the greedy horse, I still do feel you will have to take steps to control his intake before serious work if he is not to be at risk from colic caused by too much work on top of a full stomach. It is the regular work and sensible feeding which will help to get your horse fit and in good condition. Remember to clip him if he is getting hot. A blanket or trace clip will be suitable if he is out completely.

● *Mucking out is one of the many daily chores, but it can be rewarding and is an excellent way of improving your own fitness. In a busy yard large barrows are ideal*

The Partially Stabled Horse

This is perhaps the best possible method of keeping a horse. Bringing him in at night and putting him out by day, either before or after exercise, works very well for most people, and some just turn him out for a few hours; but for however long it may be, it will certainly be to his benefit as long as he settles down and is sensible. In really hot weather it may be best to reverse proceedings, and put him out at night and in, away from the flies, during the day.

This sort of routine gives the horse the best of both worlds, and having him in for part of the 24 hours will certainly help towards getting him fully fit as you can control his food intake and monitor his progress more closely. It is much easier to keep him in good condition as you can clip him out and work him harder without the worry of doing too much and getting him hot, and then having to turn him out when the weather is changeable, particularly in the autumn and winter months when he could be liable to chills.

The Stabled Horse

Fully stabled 24 hours a day, your horse is ready and waiting for whatever you want to do with it; but this doesn't mean that your life is necessarily easier! There is the daily attention, feeding, mucking out, grooming, essential exercise, shoeing and general management to organise, most of which probably has to be worked round your already busy day.

However, it is this care and attention which will help at least 50 per cent towards *your own* personal fitness, as doing your horse is hard work in itself. Mucking out a stable, whether it is straw, shavings or whatever, is strenuous and requires some fitness to be able to do quickly and efficiently. I am lucky enough not to have to 'do' my own horses any more, but I still find it useful to muck out two or three a day – pushing those wheelbarrows around does help when I am aiming towards a big event and if I feel my fitness needs improving! A few days doing this soon puts me back on course, along with a bit of running every day.

rubber glove

plastic curry comb

scissors

hoof oil

duster

body brush

rubber curry comb

tail bandage

dandy brushes

metal curry comb

mane comb

hoofpick

mane comb

● *A well-stocked grooming box with all the necessary equipment needed to keep the horse tidy*

Grooming the Stabled Horse

Grooming is good for your own fitness as well as helping to tone up the horse and stimulate his skin. Strapping in particular adds to his overall toning, and is in itself a form of exercise; it is a means of 'banging' the muscles along the neck and quarters with a rolled-up stable rubber, an action which causes the powerful muscles in these areas to contract and relax. Be sure to use a different hand for each side when you do this, rather than both sides with the same hand as some people manage to do. You will not be able to get the same feel on each side unless you use different hands.

Grooming is the one occasion when you can really spend a bit of time with your horse, looking after his needs and generally caring for him. It is essential that you get to know every lump or bump, whether these are new or old, and how or if they affect the horse and his way of going. Study your horse to see how he moves in the mornings when he first comes out of his box: does he look stiff or uncomfortable, and does he loosen up once he is moving? You should observe your horse's normal way of going, so that if anything goes wrong or he is lame at any time you know exactly what he is like normally.

Get to know how he feels after a lot of work, or if he goes lame at all after serious exertion – establish if this is a regular occurrence (in which case there is a problem), or if it was a one-off.

Feeding the Stabled Horse

Your feeding regime is particularly important with the stabled horse, as it is so easy to over-feed; far more damage will be done through over-feeding than under-feeding. Always remember to feed according to the work done, and to what suits your horse. My little Olympic horse Our Nobby, only 15hh, went round the Olympic Games in Mexico and had the second fastest round of the day on just 2lb of concentrates per day, as he was impossible to control and found everything easy; whereas Richard Meade's Cornishman was nearer 17hh and required

22lb! This does demonstrate how each animal must be treated as an individual, even when doing the same work.

There are really no hard-and-fast rules on feeding other than those already well known. Remember it is *you* who want to ride the horse, and he must feel right for the work you are giving him. He must be controllable by you, and not end up getting naughty because you are not giving him enough work. Either increase the work or lessen the food intake, not necessarily in bulk but certainly in the concentrates which are the 'hotting up' factor. If it is possible to turn the horse out regularly, this does help so much towards keeping everything calm and relaxed. A bran mash with Epsom salts given once a week will help to prevent an excessive build-up of protein and so on in the system; a mid-week mash may also tempt horses tending to get a bit 'over the top' to relax more.

How much to feed Depending on the stage of fitness of your horse, how much food in relation to work is sometimes difficult to determine, and certainly in a book it is not easy to generalise as so much is dependent on feel and experience. It is all very well saying 'If he feels and looks right then he is probably doing fine', but if you happen to be the one who has yet to *experience* that feel, you are hardly going to be able to recognise it when you have it! I have looked through dozens of books and been blinded by science and yet never come away with a cut-and-dried, proven method that would suit any or every horse.

A very rough guide is to use the height of the horse and double this to find the approximate weight in lbs that the average horse needs to maintain condition when doing average work. Thus a 16hh horse requires a total of approximately 32lb of food per day: 16 × 2 = 32lb; this includes roughage (bulk), and the total ration of roughage and concentrates should then be divided into whatever ratio you feel the horse requires. For example, a Thoroughbred type doing medium work may require a 50:50 diet – that is, 50 per cent roughage and 50 per cent concentrates. A slow half-bred may need less bulk and more concentrates to do the same amount of

● *Feeding horses is quite an art. It is vital to feed them according to the work being done, their temperament and size. Feeding the odd titbit is fine but don't make it a habit as horses soon come to expect them and get annoyed if they do not appear!*

work which because of his breeding he will find more difficult than the Thoroughbred. For example: 40 per cent roughage and 60 per cent concentrates.

A pony ridden intermittently with a not-too-ambitious child may be all right on 80 per cent roughage and 20 per cent concentrates, or even 100 per cent roughage until poor weather takes over or the pony is doing more than his food intake allows for him to maintain condition.

Clipping

For the stabled horse, clipping plays a major part in the build-up to fitness, especially during the winter months. It means that the stabled horse can be worked harder or longer without losing condition, which is what would happen if its winter coat remained and it therefore sweated a lot. It also has other advantages such as enabling you to keep the horse cleaner as grooming is easier. For the stabled horse a full, hunter or blanket clip

is ideal. Some horses feel the cold more than others, and the hunter clip (which leaves the hair on the legs) helps to protect them a little more, as well as keeping the extremities warmer. For horses doing slow work in the winter months, there is the blanket clip or high trace or racing clip, which clips the head out and generally keeps only the top of the neck and back covered; this can be ideal as it keeps the long muscles warmer and helps to prevent sweating in the usual places along neck and flanks.

It used to be said that you clipped a horse as many times as necessary before Christmas but only once afterwards, or you would ruin the new summer coat coming through. This is still true, basically, but with the strange weather patterns we have been experiencing, many horses seem to change their coats far more often than the accepted twice a year, with some either not getting a proper winter coat or never really changing to a summer one either. One of our horses changed its coat four times last year!

Rugs and Blankets

Rugs should be used on all clipped horses. It is also pointless not to use enough, as the animal will only use its stored energy reserves in keeping warm, and this is one of the quickest ways for a horse to lose condition. With so many new materials on the market there are now rugs of every weight and description suitable for every horse. Many can be put in a washing machine – although to do so too often definitely destroys some of the rug's thermal qualities.

All too often people shut the top door of the horse's stable at night, losing beneficial ventilation; in fact it would be far better if they added an extra rug and left the top door open, except in the worst weather if it is blowing into the stable. Fresh air is so important and many boxes do not have a good enough ventilation system – this is one of the main reasons that horses develop allergies and coughs, because they are not always kept in a suitable environment with free-flowing ventilation.

Most rugs nowadays have special leg straps or are specially shaped to help them

STABLE RUGS

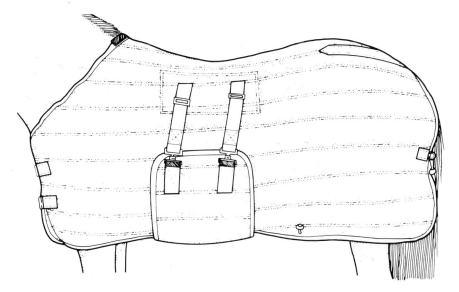

Stable rugs made of quilted nylon are light, warm and are easy to clean. They mould themselves to the shape of the horse and stay in place well.

The top example has a wide self-fabric girth attached by elasticated straps, providing extra warmth and comfort. The second version has crossing surcingles as its method of fastening.

When the rug is fitted, you should be able to fit the width of your hand easily inside the surcingles.

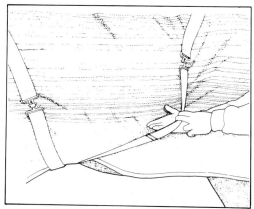

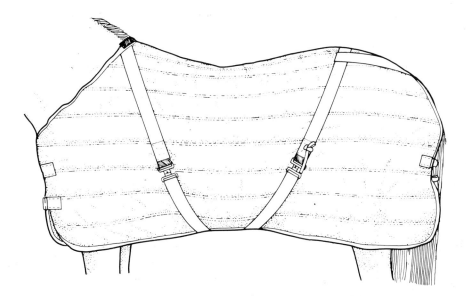

Illustrations by Sally Alexander

stay in place, so there is seldom any need for a surcingle-type roller which sometimes puts added pressure on the withers. Remember that the shaped rug needs to be at least three inches longer to compensate for the shaping. Also that in cold weather worn-out house-blankets and duvets make excellent horse blankets – there is no need to go and get an expensive new blanket if you can make do with what you already have.

Bedding Materials

Bedding must be clean and dry, and there must be enough of it to prevent the horse injuring himself when he lies down or rolls. Whatever the material used – straw, shavings, paper – it is a matter of choice, and all have their good and bad points despite everything that is written. However, I have never yet had to change a horse off straw,

● *Straw bedding is warm, free draining and light to work with. Some horses also find it rather palatable which occasionally makes it unsuitable*

which since we live on a farm is the cheapest and easiest for us to use; there are all the arguments of dust, palatability and so on, but there are usually ways round these problems. One horse definitely used to cough during mucking out when the straw was shaken, so he was taken outside for mucking out or turned out at this time. One was particularly greedy and would eat a lot of his straw, but by mucking out so that his bedding was left a little damper than normal, and with the clean straw put in the middle and with less clean on top, he did not eat so much. We tied him up an hour before riding or put a muzzle on him, and he is now eventing at Intermediate level with no ill effects and with excellent wind.

Our stables are situated on an extremely windy hill and bedding such as shavings or paper would be blown about all over the place; so although it might have been nice to have had these for one or two of the horses, the place would have looked like a rubbish tip in no time at all. Some horses, of course, really *are* badly affected by dust and if all the

● *The type of bedding used is generally a matter of choice and availability. Make sure there is enough to protect your horse from scrapes and soreness when he rolls or lies down*

the mud, exercise himself with a gallop round when he felt like it, and above all eat and drink at will if good grazing was available. The only thing he would probably thank us for would be a good shelter under which to relax if it was really hot or freezing cold or wet. Lying down and stretching out on grass seems to be the ultimate luxury for most horses – they look much more comfortable and happy outside than they ever do in the stable!

Security and Safety

Two of the most essential aspects which come into horse management are safety and security and ultimately these will affect the horse's well-being. Always spot a potential problem before it becomes a real one. All doors and gates must be securely fastened, and any gates onto roads padlocked. Some horses are amazingly adept at opening doors or gates, and will generally look extremely pleased with themselves having done so. Beware of this type of horse, because before too long they will certainly discover something else to do.

Horses that tend to get cast (roll over in their box and get stuck against the wall) should wear an anti-cast roller or be put in a bigger stable when this is less likely to happen. Always make sure there is plenty of bedding in the stable of the horse that tends to roll a lot, and that it is banked up well round the sides.

All electrical fittings should be outside the stable and either out of reach of the horse, or enclosed in piping so that it cannot be nibbled. Fire is always a potential hazard, and fires caused by an electrical fault spread alarmingly fast as the flames spread down the wires. Have a fire drill written up, with plenty of fire extinguishers at easily accessible points. Fire is always a danger in stables with so much hay and straw around, and many stables are of a wooden construction. Remember that horses tend to really panic with fire and are often difficult to move in panic situations – they have even been known to rush back towards the fire having been rescued. Get them out as quickly as possible and shut them in a field or some-

normal measures of better ventilation, soaked hay or haylage and keeping the bedding on the damp side do not work, then you will have to be advised by your vet, or you will have to leave him out for most of the time – which usually sorts out most problems, anyway!

Remember that the horse in its natural state would be roaming about loose picking at vegetation as and when it felt like it. The truth of the matter is that it is our craving to domesticate everything completely, and that alone, which drives us to coop the horse up for hours on end, to over-feed it whilst it is cooped up, to pile it with rugs and to keep it in immaculate stables, regimenting it into a routine which makes *us* feel good. All too often one feels that if the horse had his way he would be much happier running out with the natural feel of rain on his back, where he could massage himself with a good roll in

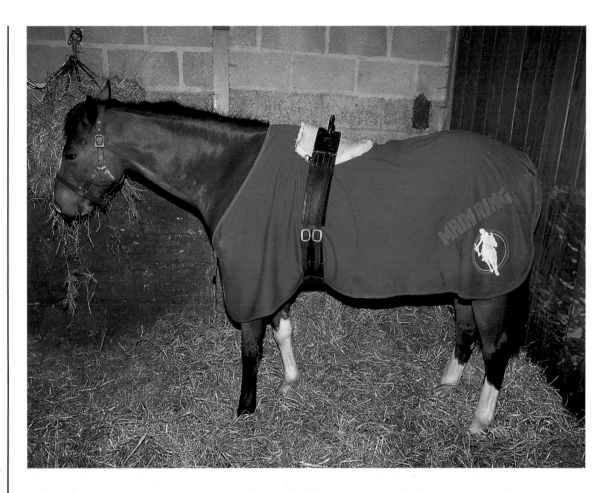

● *Some horses tend to get cast when rolling and cannot get up as they have got too close to the wall. A hooped or anti-cast roller should prevent this*

where away from the emergency. 'NO SMOKING' should be a stable rule, and should not take place anywhere within the vicinity of the stables.

Insurance gets more and more expensive, but it is certainly something worth considering very carefully. If you employ anyone to help, make sure you know the law regarding 'employer's liability'; there are, of course, advantageous concessions to all members of the British Horse Society (BHS) although not every national federation is quite so lucky. There are also leaflets and advice on all manner of problems from the BHS, which does such a great deal on the welfare side as well as for those wanting to compete. In the USA information may be obtained from the American Horse Shows Association and the American Horse Council.

Think ahead at all times, and never take unnecessary risks – the true horsemaster should be able to see sufficiently ahead to prevent accidents in many cases; but at any rate, be prepared when the unexpected happens, because it certainly will at some stage.

Monitoring Fitness

There are three main ways by which you can monitor your horse's state of health and fitness: first, by a daily taking of the temperature, pulse and respiration rates, which when read together give a good guide to your horse's health. Remember that it is essential, as with any monitoring, that you are fully aware of your horse's normal temperature before you can establish any idea of what is abnormal for that particular horse. To be successful, your monitoring should take place at the same time of day when the horse is quiet and resting to establish his normal resting rate. Once this is established you can then get a picture of how he performs at work and his recovery rate.

STABLE SAFETY

● Make sure you keep a strict safety code and always think about how to prevent accidents. Tying the horse to a drain pipe is very unsafe and could have disastrous consequences should the horse pull back

● Clipping should be done in a safe, dry area and not, as shown here, next door to the water tap

● Suitable tie rings should be used for securing horses. Fasten a loop of string through the ring, and tie the halter rope to it; if the horse pulls back for any reason the string will break, thereby preventing injury

● Horses should be tied up when mucking out. This horse could easily escape and looks as if he is just about to do so!

Temperature

Various factors will affect the horse's response to exercise, two of the main ones being heat and humidity. The horse's temperature will also be an indication of the amount of work he has done, as the temperature will rise with exercise. It will also rise, of course, if the horse is ill or has a virus, and it becomes increasingly important to know your horse's normal reactions if you want to compete seriously – only then can you establish a pattern of how he is responding to the gradually increasing workload of his fitness programme.

● *Taking the temperature is vital to monitoring a horse's state of health especially in hot and humid conditions or when illness is suspected. Make sure you keep the thermometer inserted for the correct time to get an accurate reading and always ensure it has been properly shaken down to start with*

A horse's normal temperature is generally around 38°C (100–100.5°F) but you must establish whether your horse's temperature is a little below or above this so that if he does develop a temperature you will know whether it is only a little raised, or in fact quite a lot if his 'normal' is on the low side. After strenuous exercise it will rise quite considerably, particularly if the weather is hot. Generally a horse with a temperature of over 40°C (103°F) should not be allowed to do more but must be rapidly cooled down by hosing or washing and scraping continuously with very cold water; ice can be used to good effect. It is essential that the horse is cooled quickly if damage is not to be done to vital organs. In endurance riding and three-day eventing, veterinary rules are particularly strict and careful monitoring of temperature, pulse and respiration rates takes place. Any horse who does not reach satisfactory levels in the allotted time will not be allowed to continue.

Pulse

The horse's pulse rate gives a very good reading of how the heart is responding to your fitness programme. At rest the pulse is around thirty-five to forty beats per minute, and for a horse to build up its fitness levels it is necessary for the heart to be worked hard enough to reach anaerobic levels. For this to happen the heart needs to beat approximately two hundred times a minute for a short time. The recovery rate then becomes the next most useful guide – a fit horse should have dropped down to around one-hundred-and-twenty beats per minute within a minute. It is generally accepted that the horse has possibly worked too hard if it stays above this level after the minute, and perhaps not hard enough if it is below. These are, however, only general guides and other factors such as excitement, fear, pain or fever will affect such readings.

If you possess a stethoscope, for easy reading this should be placed just in front of the girth about three to four inches above the base of the chest. Without a stethoscope the pulse is most easily read where the carotid artery passes over the cheekbone; it can also be felt in several places where an artery can be constricted against a bone.

It should be remembered that the increased heart-rate pumps more blood round the body when exercise takes place. This in turn affects the respiration rate, which also rises so as to supply more oxygen to the blood which can then remain aerobic for longer. Obviously with an unfit horse this process cannot continue for long, so gradual fitting to develop the horse's ability to withstand greater demands is an important aim.

As with humans, the horse's heart will increase in size when fit. This muscular organ weighs approximately 9lb (4kg) in a 16.1hh average hunter-type horse. It may increase by about 3lb (1.3kg) once the horse is fit – the equivalent of approximately one-and-a-half bags of sugar! If you study your horse when he first comes in off grass, and then study him again after about eight to twelve weeks of conditioning and fitness work, you will see how all his muscles have developed and strengthened, and how the fat has (or should have) noticeably disappeared.

Get into the habit of listening to your horse's heart after every workout so that you can determine how his fitness is progressing. Even if you are not doing a strenuous sport, it is worth getting to understand and know how work of any sort will affect him; then you can easily assess his fitness even if you do not want or need to do fast or really strenuous work as required for steeplechasing or even Grand Prix dressage.

There are all sorts of monitors on the market if you want to become really serious about fitness, although most of the top riders get to know how their horses are progressing by experience and feel; and once you are experienced as to what feels right it is so much easier! Never be afraid to ask knowledgeable people their advice – most are only too pleased to help. Your watch is the most useful monitor you need possess, as it can be used to count heart and breathing rate plus timing speeds over set distances if required.

Breathing

The respiration rate is an excellent indicator as to what is actually happening to your horse whilst he is working, and how he is affected by exercise. The recovery rate and how quickly breathing returns to normal after exercise is the most important factor.

At rest, the horse breathes eight to fourteen times a minute, and this is best recorded by watching the flanks – it is easy to note the in-and-out breathing motion.

You can watch the nostrils, too, although the horse at rest will not be so easy to assess in this way when quiet as compared to watching the flanks.

During exercise the respiration rate will rise dramatically, sometimes up to one-hundred-and-twenty breaths a minute. However, this should come down quite quickly once exertion is over; generally a fit horse's breathing and pulse rate will drop down within ten to fifteen minutes to comfortable limits – if left quiet, the relaxed horse will be quite normal within an hour of strenuous exercise.

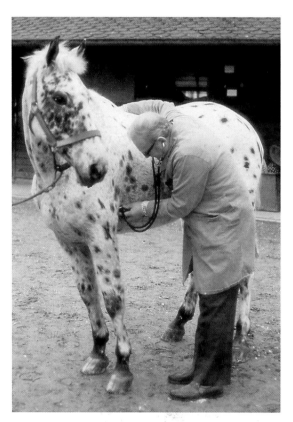

● *The easiest way of listening to the horse's heart is with a stethoscope placed on the left (near) side just behind and above the elbow. If this is not available feel for the pulse by the jawbone*

The unfit horse will take considerably longer, and it is the time limits which are important when assessing the fitness of your horse. So long as these are gradually getting less, you are on the right track. If your horse is distressed you have done too much work for his stage of fitness. Occasionally your horse may react to his work uncharacteristically, such as finishing unusually tired or

lacking the enthusiasm he showed when doing the same work as the week before. Treat this with suspicion and check him over carefully – take his temperature once he has cooled down, and see if any other signs indicate something is amiss. Never work the horse if he does not feel himself, as he may have succumbed to a virus or some other disorder; this can be confirmed by your vet, possibly with a blood test. Pushing him in such a situation could have disastrous consequences and require a long lay-off. If, however, you have a naturally lazy horse make sure he is not pulling your leg; a sharp reminder with the stick may be all that is required!

As we all know, breathing is the process whereby the animal takes in oxygen and expels carbon dioxide, and it is vital not only to existence but also to how well the horse is able to function. The more able the horse is to breathe deeply, the larger the amounts of oxygen it will be able to take in to 'feed' the muscles; this is particularly relevant when it is being asked to work hard. The shallow breathing of the unfit horse has the effect of assisting with cooling rather than taking in the larger amounts of oxygen required to convert glycogen to help 'energise' tired muscles. Once all the oxygen in the muscles is used up, the unfit horse reaches a level of fatigue known as 'anaerobic state', when the lactic acid produced in the energy conversion process builds up and effectively poisons the muscles; they are thus unable to function at a high level of work once all the glycogen energy sources are used up, or are not produced in sufficient quantity to maintain demand. Once the animal slows up, this lactic acid gradually gets removed from the muscles by the bloodstream and the fatigued horse recovers.

It is the build-up of the horse's ability to work aerobically for longer that is the basic requirement when fittening, and this can only be done by a gradual increase in the work expected of the horse.

● *Cantering is the most important pace when it comes to fitness training. How both horse and rider breathe will make a difference to the uptake of oxygen, so it is essential to relax and breathe properly in time with the movement*

Interval Training

This is an American-inspired system developed by Jack Le Goff, trainer to the American three-day event team, in the seventies and eighties and is based on the system already used by athletes and swimmers. It aims to give a specific amount of work in generally two up to five sessions with brief recovery intervals between, in which the horse only partially recovers before he is asked to work again. In this way the horse is gradually increasing his ability to do a bit more without undue stress.

Interval training has been used successfully with athletes for some years, and has also been used to good effect with horses, although there is no proof that it significantly enhances a horse's performance. However, I do believe it can be of particular benefit to the rider who has not been able to acquire that certain 'feel' that comes with experience. Its basic, scientific approach using measured distances, times and speeds

INTERVAL TRAINING
● Never start interval training until your horse has been in training for 5–6 weeks and then build up slowly.
● Always warm up slowly for a minimum of 20 minutes before commencing your interval training.
● Never do interval training more than twice a week.

Suggested start programme

Week 1	3 min canter	Week 3	3 min canter
	2 min walk		2 min walk
	3 min canter		4 min canter
	2 min walk		2 min walk
	3 min canter		4 min canter
Week 2	3 min canter		
	2 min walk		
	3 min canter		
	2 min walk		
	3 min canter		

Thereafter build up gradually over 5–6 weeks to 3 5–6 minute canters.
You can adapt this basic principle and increase either speed or time but not both according to the degree of fitness you require.

gives a certain assurance that the horse is achieving a gradual build-up of work which at least ensures that you are aiming very much in the right direction.

Basically it builds up the horse's tolerance to work, as the periods of increasing effort and the reducing rest intervals between develop the horse's capacity for more and harder work. During the rest periods the lactic acid that builds up in the muscles can be removed back into the bloodstream, and the horse returns to an aerobic state ready for more work. There are generally three work periods with two rest periods (intervals) in between, although this is sometimes increased to five plus four intervals.

Interval training is not started until stage one – your basic leg-hardening work – has been completed, and the horse is working satisfactorily out on good one-and-a-half hour hacks. To be able to get a true picture of your horse's progress it is important to keep records of what is happening. Your horse should be in good condition before you start, sound and with his shoes well fitted.

The idea is to work over a set distance in a given time. Your measured distance will need to be known, as will distances that you may add or use later as well. If you can work at a set speed over your known distance on good going this will be ideal. Start steadily in a good working trot which is approximately 220 metres per minute, and complete your course at this pace – this is the speed used in three-day eventing for the roads and tracks phase. Do this again after a short break and then straightaway take your horse's pulse rate and respiration readings. Keep your horse moving quietly for a further ten minutes, then read them again. By taking these rates both straight after work and then after a ten-minute break you can get an idea of your horse's recovery rate, and it is this rate which will tell you how fit your horse is, as he should have returned almost to normal after the ten minutes. If he has, he could do one more workout as before, therefore making it a three work and two intervals training session.

Interval training workouts are done twice a week, and are particularly helpful for the long distance and event rider. A gentle warm-up period is vital before the workouts commence – the horse should be out for at least twenty minutes before starting the training session.

By about week six to seven of your basic build-up, canter work can start and your programme can gradually increase as the horse copes with greater demands. Cantering at 350 metres per minute over a 400-metre distance would take one minute four seconds. You can work out your own distance and speeds, depending on what is available to you. If you can incorporate a slight hill into what ground you have, this will help even more towards your horse's fitness without increasing the strain to his legs.

Your programme needs to be built up gradually, first in distance and then speed. Do not increase both together – let your horse tell you when he is coping with the distance without stress, then build up your speed – but never overdo this. If you want to increase his effort, remember that the intervals in between work can be reduced, and that you can increase the number of intervals, if you want, up to a maximum of four. Your routine therefore may eventually end up being something in the region of five workouts in trot or canter, with four two- to three-minute walk periods. How far and how fast you go very much depends on what you are hoping to achieve, but the chart will give you some idea and you can adapt this depending on what you are aiming to do and the ground you have to work on.

Riding the Horse within its Fitness Limits

This is the rider's responsibility, and no horse should ever be pushed beyond what it is physically capable of doing at any time. Factors that may affect this will be its basic fitness level, its age, the weather, the ground, the type of horse, and the nature of the work asked.

Over-pushing a tired horse is inexcusable, and even an inexperienced rider should be able to feel when a horse is tiring and needs a rest. As already discussed, a horse is able to continue working after the muscles which have become anaerobic through fatigue are able to function again once the lactic acid-build-up has returned to normal. Obviously this situation will recur quite quickly if the

animal is stressed, but slow work at walk or steady trot will help the muscles to function aerobically again following mild overstressing.

Any rider with any sensitivity towards his horse should be able to sense when his mount is tiring, and should ease up pressing the horse forwards. Let the horse judge for himself at what speed or pace he feels comfortable. In very hot weather, or over hilly terrain or long distances any horse will tire. An unfit horse will tire quickly and could easily be strained physically, resulting in injury if asked to work beyond its fitness level.

The ability to pace the horse correctly for what you are hoping to achieve is not always an easy one, particularly for the inexperienced rider. In most cases you can leave the horse to find his own rhythm and then stay in balance with him, supporting him lightly between hand and leg and interfering with his way of going as little as possible. The way the rider sits and moves with the horse will make a tremendous difference; the quiet rider who sits still, straight and balanced will not interfere at all, whereas the rider swinging

● *This horse is looking tired and unenthusiastic having been pushed too far on its schooling session. Never overdo work especially with young horses: little and often is usually the best advice*

about in the saddle, on a loose rein and out of balance, crashing down on the horse's back all the time – this will take up a lot of energy from the horse, who will be having to try hard to keep his own balance to cope with the excessive movement of the rider.

The important factor in riding the horse to his best advantage is to be in balance with him at all times. Keep your position still, straight and relaxed in the saddle and allow your body to go with the movement of the horse, never against it.

Remember that young horses will tire more easily so allow for frequent breaks, following the theory of 'little and often'. They can also get tired in their backs, so avoid sitting in the same position on them for too long. Very hot weather has a dehydrating effect so give electrolytes and plenty of small drinks whenever possible.

Never gallop horses on a full stomach – take hay away for three to four hours before fast work, and allow at least an hour after feeding before taking your horse out even for a hack. If your horse gets very over-excited when competing or away from home – or even at home – avoid creating more tension by restricting him by the head. Always allow the horse to walk forwards, preferably in a circle, twisting and turning quietly to give him something to think about; and the more you can ride him on a loose rein, the more likely he is to relax. Make yourself relax physically at the same time – allow your shoulders to drop and relax, which helps the rest of your body to do so also; and this may go through to the horse and help him to relax as well.

Heat Stress

This is a word heard more and more now that people have realised the effect that hot and humid conditions can have on a horse's well-being. If the animal is competing in such conditions it may well be adversely affected unless essential steps are taken to minimise the risks involved.

During strenuous exercise the horse's temperature rises, but this is controlled by the body's own reflexes which under normal conditions keep this within safe limits. However, if the weather becomes excessively hot and humid the animal may be unable to cope with the situation and the various mechanisms involved become distorted, resulting in over-heating.

There are three main ways that the horse copes with heat: these are through sweating, the lungs and the skin. Sweating is a very effective way of cooling as evaporation takes place, ridding the body of excessive heat. One way of helping this process is to wash the horse down with cold water and scrape off the excess, allowing the body's own heat then to dry this.

Breathing itself has a cooling effect, as it allows hot air out of the body which is warmer than that breathed in. In excessively hot situations the horse may pant like a dog in its effort to assist this process, especially if for some reason its sweating mechanism

has failed – this is a known problem in hot climates.

The skin helps with heat loss by dilating the blood vessels near the surface; by increasing the circulation to these areas, it assists the heat loss mechanisms. All these processes are affected by the weather conditions: for example in cool weather it works well, and the horse will cool down quite quickly; but in hot and humid conditions when the air is already moist the horse finds itself under severe stress.

The FEI has drawn up guidelines for its competitors should heat prove to be a factor and the table provides a useful guide as to how the combined effects of heat and humidity will affect the horse:

Temperature and humidity combined	General effect
Below 54°C (130°F)	Safe to compete
Between 54°C to 66°C (130°–150°F)	Precautions should be taken
Above 82°C (180°F)	Unsuitable for competition to take place

Fat horses have a severe problem and really should not be expected to compete in adverse conditions – a fat horse can never be a fit one. It is often not realised that such things as sweat rugs, tack and a thick coat on the unclipped horse are all insulating materials and do not help the heat loss process. The less your horse carries in the form of saddle pads, numnahs, coolers, sweat rugs and so on the better in hot conditions, as all interfere with nature's most effective cooling system – that of sweating and evaporation.

Dehydration

Dehydration is one of the most damaging aspects that can affect the horse, as its body can only withstand a certain amount of fluid loss before physiological changes take place. It is most important that dehydration is kept under control and prevented whenever possible, and that fluid and electrolytes are available to the horse whenever he is in a situation where dehydration may be a factor.

This may be the case when travelling and/or competing, especially in hot weather, or when sweating is likely to occur at any time. It is essential that every rider gets to know the signs of dehydration – by using the pinch test it is easy to see for yourself the state your horse is in: take up a small fold of skin in the horse's neck, then release it – if it does not return to normal within five seconds, or if it remains pinched, your horse is suffering from dehydration caused by lack of fluid in the body. The fluid must be replaced immediately.

The horse's sweat is high in electrolytes (body mineral salts) which are essential for normal metabolism to take place. There is a

● *If the horse is very hot, cold sponging, or hosing, and the use of cold wet towels near the big veins in particular will be helpful in excessively hot weather. Natural evaporation and further cold sponging will all help to cool the horse*

much higher percentage of electrolytes in horse sweat than in human sweat, making it even more essential for these to be replaced in the horse. It is for this reason that the horse in particular is so prone to heat stress, and every precaution must be taken to ensure that dehydration with its resulting effects does not get out of control.

Most people are unaware that in hot conditions a horse may lose approximately fifteen litres (one-and-a-half buckets of water) per hour of sweat. The kidneys which control the amounts of water and electrolytes in the body can only work effectively if the volume of fluid is kept within manageable levels. If the horse loses around twenty litres or more (nearly two-and-a-half buckets of water) per hour without replacement it will suffer definite signs of dehydration and this will affect the metabolism in many ways, ultimately causing the blood to become thicker and more highly concentrated.

This in turn affects the horse's ability to cope with the heat generated by malfunctions in the body; a badly affected animal may present signs of tying up, azoturia or setfast. The respiration rate may be higher than the pulse rate as the horse tries vainly to cool itself. Because of the imbalances in the body caused by over-sweating, the horse may also be subject to involuntary quivering in the muscles and 'thumps' where the flanks seem to be acting as a pump beating. Veterinary help must be sought immediately to correct the imbalances with fluid and electrolyte replacement.

● *Dehydration can be a major problem when competing in hot and humid conditions. Make sure both you and the horse drink in such weather. Watch for dryness of the skin and lack of sweat which can indicate serious dehydration*

Coping with Heat and Humidity

Except for those competing in top level competitions, it is unlikely that the majority of riders would experience conditions likely to cause severe problems. However, it is not difficult for any horse to suffer in hot conditions, and knowing how to avoid some of the effects of riding or even living in hot and humid conditions will certainly be of great benefit to your horse.

Water must always be offered to the horse, up to within an hour of riding or competing; if possible it should be freely available at all times. Travelling is very dehydrating, so offer horses a drink on arrival, especially if it is hot. Always take water with you on a journey, plus a bucket.

Avoid getting the horse too hot by putting too many sheets or rugs on him. Cooling by evaporation is nature's way, and this is hindered by rugs or sweat sheets; only use these if there is a breeze likely to cause chilling. If possible, get into the shade or out of the sun somehow. At a competition open up every door or window in your horsebox so that the maximum amount of air is able to flow through. Keep your lorry well skipped out at

Washing down your horse and scraping him off is cooling if it is very hot, and certainly this should be done when competing, though avoid the top of the back and the loins if the water is very cold as this could cause stiffness in the back muscles. It is the water evaporating after scraping that really cools the horse, so if he is still hot once he is dry repeat the process.

Placing a cold wet towel over the poll and down the neck is refreshing *whilst it remains cold* but remove it as soon as it is no longer effective. An excellent way of cooling is, of course, to hose the horse down if this facility is available. Ice (if available) should also be used if necessary.

If you know you are going to experience hot conditions it is worth giving your horse electrolytes over this period; however, never put these in the horse's water unless he is used to them in case it puts him off drinking altogether. It is best sprinkled on a feed and mixed in well. There is no point in giving electrolytes when it is not hot, or over too long a period prior to exertion in the heat, as

● *Gently stroking the ears is soothing and helps to warm the horse. This is the best method of telling if your horse is warm enough: warm ears indicate a warm horse, cold ears a cold one*

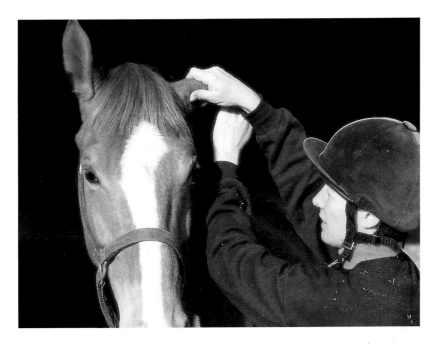

this can cause an imbalance which may adversely affect the horse; use them only to *replace* body salts lost in sweating, and do not overload the system for too long before exertion is going to take place. However, electrolytes can certainly be started the day before a major event and continued for a few days afterwards. Salt should always be available to the horse in the form of a salt lick.

One of the best ways of stimulating the horse's body system to work effectively is by keeping him moving after exertion. If he is very hot he should be sponged down on the move so that the lactic acid in the muscles is encouraged to disperse, and not allowed to build up in static tired muscle fibres. Frequent drinks once he has cooled sufficiently are essential until he is satisfied.

Always keep an eye on your horse after exertion, and check that he has not broken out in a cold sweat, which is an indication that there are still painful deposits left in the muscles. Walking out in hand is the best way to help disperse these, and it is soothing and comforting to rub the ears which are often cold and wet – if they really are cold he will definitely benefit from having them gently rubbed because rather like humans trying to sleep when they have cold feet, the horse is invariably uncomfortable if he has cold ears. Walking him and rubbing his ears therefore really does seem to help settle him

after a hard day's work, whether it has been hot or not.

Give just a small feed but only when he has settled, then give another later on. It is very easy to put horses off their feed by overfacing them when they are tired. Do the pinch test, and if there are no signs of dehydration, fine – but if there are, add electrolytes to the feed or water if they're used to it.

When travelling home after a stressful competition in hot conditions it is important to stop and offer water at intervals, especially if it is a long journey. Different horses will react differently to the stress of a competition regardless of the conditions, but those affected by heat will need to be carefully watched as the worried horse inevitably takes much more out of itself than one with a calmer disposition.

As with most things in life, common sense plays a major part in the successful management of horses: if you were to stop and consider what *you* might require if you were the horse, most things would become fairly obvious! The difficulty is doing these things in the right order and with the minimum of fuss. However, riding your horse within his fitness limits remains the most vital aspect, whether it is hot or not. Know your horse, know what you can expect of him, and then ride him in such a way that you can achieve the goal you have set yourself at that time.

5  THE SPECIFIC DISCIPLINES

By this stage you should be well on the way to having a lot of fun out of your riding and will, I hope, have competed in several events at your chosen sport. If you have done your homework and given your horse and yourself every chance and enough time, your fitness programme should be on target.

Rider Fitness

Have you found any problems to date? The most common are usually predictable, such as getting tired, aches and pains, sores on the legs; others might be an inability to progress, nervousness and lack of confidence – or perhaps the opposite: over-confidence, which sometimes leads to unnecessary falls. Maybe the horse is lame or has lost condition; perhaps you do not have enough knowledge of your chosen sport and are afraid of making a fool of yourself: this can also mean progress is not being made.

Tiredness is only to be expected until you have ridden progressively for some weeks or even months. However, remember that riding is quite an arduous sport and it is important that you eat sensibly; although everyone's metabolism is different, a high energy diet is essential if you are to be able to maintain and progress towards ultimate fitness. Check you are eating enough of the right food, and give yourself a chance. Take a snack with you if you are going off on a long ride – it is easy to take something in your pocket or in a small knapsack if it is likely to be a long day. A mini first-aid kit could be in the same bag.

It is no good being overweight: there is no doubt that those who are tire more easily, nor does this and good riding go together –

you will not be effective if you have too much flab. So, keep this under control and do not allow it to creep up. Everyone has their own way of losing weight but remember that everything in moderation is as good a system as any; crash diets and cutting things out altogether seldom provide a long-term cure. Eat sensibly: plenty of salads, fish and lean meat and fruit rather than too many potatoes, puddings, chocolates and biscuits.

I personally find it very easy to lose weight if I cut down on my fluid intake – as a rule I have far too many cups of tea and coffee during the day. Perhaps you have this tendency too; although as a rider you do need plenty to drink in hot weather, like the horse. It is better to eat a little less of everything, rather than to stop certain foods altogether; and rather than pick at biscuits and sweets, try apples and carrots – and your horse can have the bits you don't want!

Exercise burns up calories, but if you eat more than you burn up you will put on weight. Having said that, it is worth noting that muscle is slightly heavier than fat, so if you are using up energy and developing muscle you may also get a slight increase – although this sort of weight increase goes hand in hand with a fitter, trimmer figure.

Do not forget that you need rest and relaxation just as much as healthy exercise; some people require a lot more sleep than others, but it is important that you are able to get the sleep you need. If you are one of those

● *Three-day eventing is one of the most strenuous of equestrian sports. It requires a very high degree of fitness from both horse and rider, and it takes three to five years to train a horse sufficiently to compete at Badminton, the world's biggest three-day event*

unlucky people who find sleeping difficult, make sure that you have tried all the usual tips such as:

- Make your room as dark as possible – eye shades can be very helpful.
- Have a light meal and/or warm drink before retiring.
- Relax in a bath and try to forget the day's worries, or go for a walk, or read a book before bed.
- Train yourself to relax, and mentally think of sleep before you retire.
- Switch off from the day's worries.

If you are not progressing with your riding or your fitness for the sport, spend a little time analysing why this is so. Are you getting the necessary help? – so often when things are not going quite according to plan it is something very minor. It may just be the wrong technique that is holding you back, or maybe you have done a bit too much too soon and your confidence is a bit shaken. Sometimes it is your saddle that is putting you in the wrong position for what is comfortable; some people do not feel happy or secure in certain saddles, especially if they are rather straight cut.

If you have tried the exercises mentioned so far to help your own riding fitness, you shouldn't really have a problem with this aspect; but if you have, then it may well be that you are not breathing properly during your ride; that you are aiming too high; or are perhaps suffering from a virus or something yourself and so are just not feeling as good as you might.

The following pages give advice on how to prepare you and your horse for specific activities. All basic fitness work – stage one – starts out the same for all, with slow conditioning work to build up muscle and help the heart and lungs to work more effectively, although different trainers have different ideas as to whether this should be done on the road or in a field and along tracks. The second phase includes schooling specific to whatever you aim to do ultimately, but must include suppling exercises. The third stage is the fine-tuning in preparation for the competitions in mind.

The Dressage Horse

Dressage is becoming an extremely popular discipline; it follows the most classical principles of riding and is the basis for many other activities. The word 'dressage' came from the French word *dresser* meaning 'training' and this is exactly what it is. In following a recognised programme of schooling exercises the horse becomes sufficiently supple, loose and flexible in his muscles and frame to perform the many and varied movements demanded for the various levels required. According to the rule books, the objective is 'the harmonious development of the physique and ability of the horse'; this should lead to the horse being 'confident, attentive and keen' whilst remaining calm but obedient to the rider's wishes.

Every rider should have some basic knowledge of what is required to make a horse go willingly forwards, to keep straight, turn and remain under control; however, the dressage rider requires a much more comprehensive knowledge of what the horse is physically capable of doing and how to set about persuading it to do so. Confidence is vital, so each stage in training must be achieved patiently; in many dressage movements the horse is expected to do more than he is capable of naturally, and so he must fully understand what is expected. Therefore one of the basic principles of training is to repeat a movement until it is perfected – on both reins, of course.

The fitness required for the dressage horse is very different from that required for the eventer, show jumper or point-to-pointer. It is muscle power that needs to be developed more than the heart and lungs, which are not worked to the same degree as in galloping horses. As the dressage horse improves and performs more collected work, its centre of balance will move further back; the development of the hindquarters becomes more obvious, and the neck and top line should become more pronounced. Because of the time it takes to build up this muscle and power, it would be self-defeating to compromise what has been achieved by letting the dressage horse right down, as is generally the custom with horses that have more demanding work to the legs such as jumpers and eventers. The dressage horse therefore usually stays in work throughout the year with just two or three short holidays so that muscle tone is not lost.

Since dressage is such a very disciplined type of work, the dressage horse must be allowed to have plenty of relaxation and fun alongside training. There is nothing worse than seeing a horse doing a test as if he were a robot, looking demoralised and depressed, and it is perhaps the one sport where it is essential to add variation to your schooling such as fun hacks out, a little jumping training and gridwork. And there is no reason at all why the dressage horse should not have a bit of faster work to develop his heart and lungs – certainly my sister, Jennie Loriston-Clarke, and Dutch Courage, Britain's world bronze medallist, would join me for fast work on occasions, even though he would not go the whole distance or necessarily the same speed when the training session was nearing a three-day event. Dutch Courage loved it, and would then do superb passage on the way home!

It can take up to six years for the horse to develop the power and ability to perform at Grand Prix levels in dressage. All the early work must aim towards a progressive build-up of muscle and power; even in his road-work the horse must be encouraged to use himself well – he must be active and purposeful, and asked to work on the bit early in the fitness programme.

Most dressage horses are trained in a school, and it is very easy to overdo things with muscles that are still young, or not toned up enough to cope with the demands of the rider. So often problems develop at this early stage because the horse has been worked a little too hard and has perhaps slightly strained a muscle – this might be so minor that it is not really noticeable, but for the unfortunate horse unable to tell us much, it may be quite uncomfortable to turn in one direction or another. Thus he protects himself by tensing up against the hurt, and so becomes one-sided or evades or resists certain demands. Probably only the most discerning rider will be able to assess that all is not well in such a situation, as the feeling

● *The dressage horse has to be trained in the correct basic techniques from an early age in order to progress properly through the various levels. Not all horses have the ability, temperament or willingness to become top dressage horses but with patience and perseverance a lot of fun can be had from this absorbing sport*

will be very slight. Your horse 'back man' may be able to tell you where the problem is and treat it; very often a week's rest will be all that is required – a few days in the field to relax and stretch muscles without the weight of the rider can work wonders, especially for youngsters.

When schooling the dressage horse, the initial period of loosening and suppling-up work is essential, and this should never be hurried, especially with the horse working at medium level or above. Similarly at the end of a workout a certain period of time should be spent to allow the horse to relax and wind down. If you always do this he will come out much better the next day. Dressage is all about looseness, and too often one sees horses being prepared with too little time spent on the basics.

Build up your work gradually and spend a little more time each week or month on the aspects that need improving so that you are fittening your horse by increasing demands.

Remember that the young or sensitive horse must never be expected to do too much; if things are not going well it is usually best to have a break or do something else, and then come back to the exercise you were finding difficult.

If a horse has been off work for a while it is still important to build up his work *gradually* over a few weeks – even the advanced horse will find it strenuous to go straight back into a full-time training programme, particularly doing such movements as piaffe, passage and canter pirouettes.

If your horse is getting heavy in the hand this usually means you need more leg to push him up off his forehand. Vary your work more, with more emphasis on transitions from one pace to another, or within the paces from collected to medium or extended. Again, stiffness is usually caused by the horse bearing down and leaning on the rider's hand: he must be pushed up in front with a stronger leg and seat, and then kept loose and supple with a sensitive hand.

Correct lungeing can be very beneficial to both the horse and the rider if problems persist; so many faults can be corrected if the horse goes willingly forwards into the side-reins in rhythm and with collection. He will soon find his own balance, and other problems will sort themselves out as he gains confidence and starts to loosen and work properly. However, be careful not to overdo lungeing work by failing to give the horse a good break on a loose rein so that he can relax and stretch all his muscles. It is just as important to give the horse a break when lungeing as it is when you are riding him.

The Dressage Rider

The serious dressage rider will need to practise as much work without stirrups as possible, as this helps to develop a deep and effective seat. Think about your own straightness in the saddle and your overall position. Trot and canter so that you are

● *The position of the rider is particularly important for the dressage rider. Straightness, balance and co-ordination must be worked at, and riding without stirrups on the lunge is one of the best ways to achieve this. This rider, under the watchful eye of her trainer, is learning how to stay in balance whilst doing arm exercises without stirrups*

pushing yourself as much as possible, but without tensing up against the work. Make yourself relax, but keep your muscles working in rhythm with the horse and allow your back to 'give' in time with this. Keep your legs on your horse so that he is working 'between your hands and legs' and maintains forwardness and lightness on the bit.

During the transitions from one pace to another be sure to maintain your position – it is easy to allow your weight to move and let your lower leg flop back and forth. Keep yourself upright but in balance at all times; the classic mistake is to allow yourself to lean back too much. If in doubt come forwards, regain your balance and then sit up more afterwards. Your lower leg should act as your roots: firm and strong, supporting the trunk or upper body. If this is strongly in place it will be easy to maintain balance, and the rest of the body will be able to adopt its

● *Jennie Loriston-Clarke and Dutch Courage, Britain's only dressage medallists to date (Bronze at the World Championships in 1978 performing the Piaffe – the most collected of all movements) trotting on the spot. To reach Grand Prix levels the horse requires years of training to build up sufficient muscle to be able to perform the movements required with grace and ease*

own position naturally in the saddle.

For the dressage rider, the more time actually spent in the saddle the better; obviously keep up any of the basic fitness exercises you find helpful, both on or off the horse, but it is the riding – especially without stirrups – that will help most. It is not unknown for many riders to do all their schooling without stirrups. Ten minutes might seem an age to start with, but by the time you can cope with a whole hour without getting 'floppy' you will know that you are right on target for peak fitness!

The Event Horse

The event horse enjoys greater variety in its discipline, but this does require a high degree of fitness if it is to cope with the demands of the sport. The dressage helps to school the horse for the two jumping phases, the cross-country and the show jumping: these in turn are rather different, the former requiring speed and quickness over the fences, the latter accuracy and precision to achieve those elusive clear rounds.

In the three-day event there is also the endurance factor, which demands tremendous fitness in both horse and rider if the best is to be obtained from the horse by the rider. The slow build-up of fitness, taking weeks and months, is essential if the horse is to be able to cope with what is required without being overstressed. The variety of the work and the need for increasing the horse's endurance ability does ensure that most event horses are given a good grounding in most of their work. However, some people do tend to over-gallop their horses in the misguided belief that fast work is the only way to get them fit. Certainly for steeplechasing and top level eventing the horse *does* need to be given enough galloping to ensure it can cope with anaerobic work for progressive periods; however, a great deal of galloping is seldom needed below three-day event standard.

Basic fitness *must* be achieved before asking the horse to do any jumping or faster work. Spend time on flatwork before progressing to gridwork, and always warm up enough before asking the horse to do anything strenuous. Remember, you are basically dealing with an endurance sport and the horse must be in good condition for this, not too thin, nor too fat which would add strain to his legs and heart. Never gallop an over-fat horse. With the greedy type you will have to harden your heart and be quite ruthless about cutting down his bulk intake, spreading out his rations during the day. If he eats his bedding a lot you may have to change this to paper or shavings.

The event horse needs plenty of exercise and will benefit from being turned out whenever possible, especially if he tends to get a bit uptight as he gets fitter. Leading out in hand for some grass may be of benefit if turning out is difficult. Some people like to ride twice a day, but while this might be nice in theory, not many can spare the time; there is also the other aspect of giving the horse enough chance to relax and rest. This may be easy in a small yard but there is little rest anyway for those in a busy yard. Besides, if the work you give the horse has been properly carried out, he should be well worked in relation to the food he is getting.

Never forget to check the state of your horse's feet *regularly*. The eventer has a tough time training and competing over difficult ground, so be sure to keep his feet and shoes in good shape – never let a loose shoe do 'one more day' as it might cause an injury that could put you out of action for weeks.

Train your event horse to go on all surfaces and to cope both up and down hills. He must be confident and balanced to canter up and down gradients both when jumping or out hacking. You will also have to adjust your work to suit different types of horse, and so you can aim your training programme towards the level at which you are wanting to compete. The Novice eventer has to cope with the dressage and show jumping tests, followed by a one-and-a-half mile cross-country of up to twenty fences in one-day events. This requires a fit horse, but if ridden sensibly it is not too demanding.

The horse aiming for Intermediate or Advanced one-day eventing is doing more demanding dressage and jumping tests as well as a longer and stiffer cross-country, probably just over two miles for Intermediate and around two-and-a-half miles for Advanced with between twenty-two and twenty-eight fences. Courses may be hilly or fairly flat, but anyway are going to require a fitter horse than for Novice level, so your work-to-food ratio will need assessing to make sure the horse does not lose condition, and that he copes with the demands made on him.

Your training programme must allow time for problems associated with the weather, especially in the winter months when snow or frost can severely disrupt your training. For those aiming for a three-day event it is

important to appreciate what the horse will actually have to do, so that you are fully aware of the distances involved and the jumping efforts required as well as the speeds.

The speed and endurance test on the second day of a three-day event is divided into four phases, the first and third of these, phases A and C, being roads and tracks. Phase A is a warm-up for the steeplechase, and can be anything between three to six kilometres ridden at an optimum speed of 220 metres per minute; this works out at a strong trot pace or steady canter, covering approximately one kilometre in four minutes.

Phase B is steeplechase and the fastest phase, run round a course of four to ten steeplechase fences over approximately one to two-and-a-half miles at an optimum speed of between 640 to 690 metres per minute, depending on the standard of the event. The horse is therefore required to jump safely at speed – this may be easy for the Thoroughbred but can prove a problem for

● *Gridwork is one of the best ways of teaching horse and rider how to cope with situations in quick succession. Both have to adapt quickly to the variety of fences sited so closely together*

the heavier types. Never push your horse too fast out of his rhythm, as this is when damage is done and falls or injuries occur.

Phase C consists of further roads and tracks, so the horse can wind down after the steeplechase. Contrary to some misguided belief, the longer this is, the greater is the horse's chance of recovery before he tackles the most demanding of the phases, the cross-country. Phase C is usually between five and ten kilometres long, and also to be carried out at 220 metres per minute.

Phase D is the cross country, though before a horse may start there is a ten-minute compulsory halt when he is inspected by a veterinary panel; he may only continue on Phase D if he is considered fit (pulse and respiration readings) and sound (trot-up) enough to do so. The course for Phase D is between two to three miles, over twenty or thirty obstacles, to be ridden at speeds ranging from 520 to 570 metres per minute. At Advanced level this becomes extremely demanding, requiring a very high degree of fitness. One might consider that at Novice level it is equally demanding, though in a different sense, because although the course for the Novice horse is not as far or as fast, he has probably never reached this degree of fitness before and will be feeling the effects of this as he copes with his most difficult task to date.

Horses that have once achieved a high degree of fitness undoubtedly come back to that state much more quickly the second and subsequent times. I have often found it extremely difficult to feel satisfied with the fitness of a Novice horse doing his first serious event or three-day event, and usually make it a rule that we go more for a happy school than as a serious competition; this is because one just has no idea how the horse is going to react or respond to the demands of the competition. I have also always strongly believed that first experiences make a big impression and should be easy and uncomplicated. I therefore try not to put young horses under too much pressure, and certainly do not go out to win until they know what the sport is all about – although having said that, if I have a really talented horse which has found the preparation easy, I will not be holding him back!

The following charts give some guidelines on the work that might be given to horses competing at different levels – though never forget that your horse is an individual, and there are no hard-and-fast rules. The only really important one is to be conscientious in your early fitness work, as this is vital to long-term soundness and condition.

The ultimate aim when training for eventing is to develop the horse's muscles, heart and lungs to function at maximum efficiency; this is achieved by covering gradually increased distances at a steady strong canter. The event horse rarely needs to gallop,

● *Galloping at speed is a technique that should be practised before riding the steeplechase phase of a three-day event. This bullfinch fence serves as a suitable substitute for a steeplechase fence. For this type of riding the stirrups should be shorter and a firm feel should be maintained on the reins*

but he does need to work strongly. He could start this cantering work once his basic slow work and schooling phases were well under way. The first workout would be cantering strongly for half to three-quarters of a mile on the flat, maybe less if the distance included a hill. After a couple of sessions like this and when the horse feels comfortable, you could go further, up to a mile – the last half mile can be ridden on more strongly.

If you are doing two canter workouts a week, one should be strong work and the other kept steady so that you are not over-straining the horse. Horses that are good in their wind and find the work easy will probably only need one good canter a week; the stuffier horse, or those that find cantering hard work inevitably need more of it to reach peak fitness. Keep a firm contact, and keep him in balance when working him. Always check the horse's legs carefully before a training workout to ensure there is no heat anywhere; if ever you feel they are not a pair, or if the horse feels out of sorts, do *not* do any fast work. Watch him carefully in case a problem is developing and continue your programme only when you are sure all is well.

GUIDELINE CHARTS ON FITNESS FOR ONE-AND THREE-DAY EVENTS

NOVICE 1-DAY EVENT

WEEKS	STAGE 1 – SLOW WORK	STAGE II – SCHOOLING	STAGE III FAST WORK
1	Walking ½–1hr		
2	Walking 1–1½hrs		
3	Walk & Trot 1–1½hrs		
4	Walk & Trot 1–2hrs	20 mins x 2 per week	
5	Short Hack Daily	Flat Work x 3 per week	
6	Hacks or Slow Trot	+ Flat Work – Grids	Slow Long Canters
7	Hacks or Slow Trot	Flat Work Jumping x 2	½ speed Gallop 1 or 2
8	Hacks or Schooling	X.C. School	Competition

NOVICE 3-DAY EVENT

WEEKS	STAGE 1 – SLOW WORK	STAGE II – BUILD UP	STAGE III TUNE UP
1	Walking ½–1hr		
2	Walking 1–1½hrs		
3	Walk & Slow Trot 1–1½hrs		
4	Walk & Slow Trot 1–2hrs		
5	Walk & Slow Trot 1hr or Short Hack	+ Flat Work x 2 per week	
6	Slow Work or Hack	+ Flat Work & Cantering	
7	Hacks & Hills	Schooling Flat & Grids	Slow Canters X.C. School
8	Hacks & Hills	Jumping – Fast Work x 1	Schooling – IDE (Slowly)
9	Easy for 2–3 days Hacks & Hills	Show Jumping – Fast work	Fast Work or 1-Day Event (Faster)
10	Easy for 2–3 days Longer Hacks 1½–2hrs	Schooling – Fast work	Fast Work or 1-Day Event
11	Easy if evented Long Hacks & Hills	Put Right Any Problems Schooling	Easy – After 1 Good Gallop at Weekend
12	Easy Relaying Hacks	Brief Schooling – Keep Happy	3-DAY EVENT

All horses should have a day off a week and be turned out as much as possible throughout their training.

The Event Rider

The event rider needs to be very fit to compete, especially if he is to cope satisfactorily with the cross-country phase. There is no better way of achieving fitness than by riding regularly, but it is most important that you are sufficiently fit to help your horse and to ride him as well as you possibly can should he start to get tired at the end of a cross-country course. If you ride regularly and are an active, fit person anyway you will find it easy, but not everyone is able to lead an active outdoor life or to ride every day, even when they want to compete.

To improve your own fitness, use whatever form of exercise you find most helpful, though remember you need to develop your own heart and lungs as well as the relevant muscles so as to be able to ride your horse effectively. It is essential for you to ride and school at both dressage and jumping so as to accustom yourself to the different positions required; also to shorten your stirrups right up to gallop or canter your horse, so you know you are breathing correctly and that your legs and back muscles are in trim. At the other extreme, work without stirrups always helps fitness.

Be sure you can control your horse – it is too late to discover you cannot stop on the day of the competition and dangerous for you both. In the excitement of the event and particularly when galloping across country your horse may get stronger than he has felt before. After one or two competitions he may also start to realise only too well what the routine is, and getting into that start-box becomes the signal for a gallop. However, safety must always be paramount in your mind, and a stronger bit may be necessary until your horse has settled – which he probably will do after three or four events.

In the lead-up to an event a bit of running can certainly help to clear the rider's wind. Eat a healthy diet with energy-giving foods, and try to remember how important it is to nourish your body *especially* before you compete, however much your nerves are getting to you! Have a bowl of cereal, piece of toast and marmalade, a banana, *anything* – but give yourself a chance and make yourself have something at the beginning of the day before you set off. In hot weather particularly have plenty to drink, preferably with electrolytes as well as giving them to your horse!

The Show Jumper

Show jumping is a specialist sport and the horse must have regular training to develop its technique to maximum efficiency and effect. Most of the early work is done on the flat, teaching the horse balance and obedience and developing his strength in the quarters and hocks.

Fitness exercise for the show-jumping horse is worked in with his training, and he does need regular sessions to be able to cope with the big fences met at top levels; always, training must aim to develop technique. It is the canter which is so important for the show jumper, as he must have the balance and power in his canter to extend and

● *Hours of work over poles and fences will help the horse to perfect his footwork and neatness when it comes to jumping bigger fences*

shorten the stride as required, and so he can spring off the ground more easily. Transitions and halts are the best schooling movements to help the horse shift his power and his centre of gravity further back so that he can do this.

The horse must be responsive and accept the bit: to this end, the rider must have light hands and a strong leg so that the horse is confident of going forwards into the hand. The rider above all must be consistent in his riding – it is no good asking the horse to go in deep to a fence on one occasion, then ask him to stand off at the next. Of course there are occasions when both will be required, but to build up the necessary confidence consistency is vital.

Freedom over the fence is also vital – be sure you do not interfere with the horse's

● *Show jumping requires athleticism and correct techniques to be really successful. The rider needs co-ordination, good balance and a sense of timing to help his horse to the maximum. A dedicated approach and correct training as you progress through the different levels is important*

jump in any way: it is essential to be in balance at all times, neither getting in front of the movement, nor behind it so that your weight on the saddle causes the horse to knock a fence behind. If you catch the horse in the mouth *at all* the freedom of his jump will almost certainly be compromised.

Schooling over fences is important to build up confidence between horse and rider, and this in itself (after the initial slow work) should get your horse fit enough for the ring, as you will be doing the same type of work in competition. However, I sincerely believe that all horses need variation in their work to keep them fresh and interested, and I feel sure that if show jumpers did some cross-country schooling and learned to jump ditches, banks, trakhenas and so on, it would be beneficial for them – especially when they reach the big time, such as at Hickstead. Every horse needs to see a bit of everything before he is made to specialise in any one discipline. The only type of cross-country fence I would avoid with the show jumper would be jumping into water. For his sport he only ever has to jump *over* it, so

it would seem sensible just to jump big ditches and open water, rather than confuse the issue and make him go in – something you certainly do *not* want from the show jumper!

In general, show jumpers do not do as much gridwork as the eventer who has a wider variety of fences to get accustomed to, but some is definitely beneficial, and it is particularly useful with young horses as it teaches them about combinations. Grids can also be useful to teach the horse to lengthen and shorten his stride through combination fences.

As with every type of training, never overdo any one part of your training, and be sure to work and jump only on good ground – nothing will put the jumping horse off quicker than to be asked to jump big fences on hard ground. He will quickly start to shorten his stride, which will mean combination distances will be difficult to achieve – the whole thing could end in disaster if you do not think about such things and act accordingly. Save your horse for another day if the ground is too hard. Nothing will make up for spoiling a young horse's enjoyment of the sport once he has started to think that it might not be such fun after all.

● *A variation in the grids jumped is important to teach the horse to be alert. Always start small and don't confront the horse with a sea of poles in the early stages*

The Show-jumping Rider

The rider of the show-jumping horse must keep fit and alert, and be able to make the best decisions on the day; physically he must also be in good condition so that he can work with his horse and ride him to the best of his ability. Most important is to keep to the correct course – it is no good missing fences out because you have forgotten the order of fences. Make yourself learn it, and if this is a particular weakness, go out and practise over as many different courses as possible until this has improved. Things are always worse under stress, so you need to get your brain working and in tune with what you are doing long before you reach the stage of being, say, in a team – you won't be very popular with other team-mates if you let them down by losing your way. Human nature being what it is, they will soon forget your good performances but they will never forget your mistake!

It is important to breathe properly

● *This rider has a good firm leg position but has flung her weight forward which could push the horse onto its forehand. She is, however, looking ahead to the next fence*

throughout your competition round, taking in enough oxygen to keep a clear head so that you can make quick decisions. At home, practise turning off corners so that you keep your mind and reactions alert on whether to push on or take a little more control in front of a fence. Things happen quickly in show jumping and it is important that you keep ahead of everything.

Show jumping involves a great deal of hanging around between classes, and it is too easy to get into the habit of eating and drinking while you wait – it is quite noticeable how some show jumpers soon end up looking rather large! The world champion or Olympic medallist can obviously cope, but for those ordinary mortals still trying to reach the top I would suggest you keep your weight down. In fact whatever sport you

● *The approach to this fence is spoilt by the rider having too long a leather for jumping. In her efforts to keep the leg on, the heel has come up and she is likely to tip forward over the actual jump and support herself on her hands. She is offering the horse freedom with her hands*

● *This rider is in a very nice position. Her weight is down in her heel, she is off the horse's back and has given her hands sufficiently to allow the horse to stretch forwards and round well over the jump*

take part in, you will basically be in better shape to do your best if you keep near your ideal weight – for the rider, the horse will appreciate your efforts anyway, and your reflexes will undoubtedly be that fraction quicker which might make all the difference in a jump-off against the clock.

Long Distance Riding

This is a most popular sport, and for many people who do not necessarily have either the time or the inclination to follow more competitive events, it is one at which they can excel. Both horse and rider have to be extremely fit, and it takes a lot of hard work and planning to compete the various rides of forty miles or more successfully.

Basically the long distance horse requires a longer, slower preparation than most other competition horses, the aim being to build up strength and stamina, which all takes time. The rider must be extremely fit as well so that he can help the horse when he is getting tired – there can be no greater hindrance than a tired rider flopping about in the saddle. Sloppy riding could also lead to saddle sores, or even lameness if all the weight is on one side.

More than other competitors in any other discipline long distance riders are highly aware of cardiovascular problems and treat their horses' heart and breathing rates very seriously. Generally the pulse rate may be double or even treble the breathing rate in normal conditions; these readings are taken regularly and treated very seriously if anything appears amiss.

Muscular stress is another problem: this occurs in a tired horse, and the pace must be steadied to prevent exhaustion. The horse will stumble and lose co-ordination, and muscle tremors are sometimes seen. The rider must also watch carefully for signs of dehydration, especially in hot weather, for setfast or for colic, all of which might be provoked by metabolic disturbances during a long ride.

The long distance horse does not have to go fast but he must maintain a steady pace for long distances; he will therefore benefit from more time spent at the slow stage doing

walk and trot. This will certainly increase general fitness overall and harden tendons and muscles, and it is always good for any horse to allow longer over the general conditioning process. At the end of this time you are likely to be doing up to two-and-a-half to three hours a day if time permits.

Always bear in mind what it is you are aiming for, as it is in the horse's best interests if he is accustomed to doing what is ultimately going to be expected of him. Building up your rides over varied ground will help

your horse to be sure-footed and alert as well as to develop muscle. A little hill-work is always good, but it is unlikely that the endurance horse will meet many severe hills so this is not essential. However, it *is* important to make the horse work – he must not be allowed to slop along but must be made to use himself if he is to improve his overall state of condition.

How fit the horse must be depends on the standard of ride you are aiming for – for example, it is generally accepted that a horse

● *Long distance riding is very popular but requires a high standard of fitness and horse management skills. The horse must be carefully prepared and encouraged to drink along the way*

ready to go hunting would be fit enough to do a short ride of around twenty miles with few ill-effects. It must be remembered, however, that the hunter is not expected to keep going for too long, having various checks during the day, whereas the endurance horse must keep up its steady pace.

● *Riders often dismount during endurance rides to rest their horses, but it is essential that they work on their own fitness with as much enthusiasm as that of their horses*

Generally it is known that a basically fit horse would be able to do the following distances as long as he had put in a certain amount of extra fitness work, according to the length of the ride.

20 miles = plus two weeks extra fitness work
40 miles = plus seven to eight weeks extra fitness work
60 miles = plus eleven to twelve weeks extra fitness work
75 miles = plus fifteen to eighteen weeks extra fitness work
100 miles = plus twenty weeks extra fitness work

The horse's paces (and therefore distance covered per hour) will vary according to his length of stride; if he is short-striding, in particular, you must keep pushing him on so that he develops a more swinging stride. The following chart will give you a rough idea of what times you should be able to achieve at the different paces:

Walk = four to five miles per hour
Slow trot = six to seven miles per hour
Strong trot = nine to ten miles per hour
Flowing canter = ten to twelve miles per hour

You can vary your work with a bit of faster work, but in order not to overstress your horse, the average overall time should not exceed ten to twelve miles per hour.

It is important to know at what pace and speed your horse feels most comfortable, because it is in this that he will ultimately feel happiest. When trotting, be sure to change the diagonal frequently: this pace is generally the most commonly used, although it very much depends on what your horse finds most restful and easy.

Because of the varying distances it is important that the horse is prepared for the distance being aimed for: thus for a forty-mile ride the horse must be trained towards this distance – and as with everything in endurance riding, it is the long, slow preliminary work which is so essential. Only in this way can the horse build up the slow twitch muscles so rich in oxygen, and which therefore tire only slowly because they increase their aerobic capacity. To help develop this capacity, a certain amount of fast work should be included in the training routine; interval training has proved useful for this, once a good, basic fitness programme has been in practice for some time.

The qualifying rides are an excellent indicator as to how both horse and rider are getting on and if the required speeds are being achieved easily; you will be able to judge if things are progressing satisfactorily, and whether the horse is being sufficiently carefully watched and monitored in his training. There is no doubt that some horses find the distance and speed easier than others, therefore some will require more work in their preparations.

Always ask for help and advice from those who are already competing and keep a record of what you are doing and how far you still have to go. It is impossible to give specific guidelines on how you should train your horse, but after the first few weeks of basic work you should be building up so that during the week you are doing at least one-and-a-half to two hours of work per day at six to seven miles per hour, plus one day's faster work, at around ten miles per hour. Two of these workouts should cover approximately twenty to twenty-five miles at around seven miles per hour. Do not, however, overdo things with your horse during the week before competing – it is better to ease off a little at this stage.

There are various types of ride – the pleasure ride, the competitive trail ride and the

● *The back-up team is a vital part of the management when endurance riding. Frequent drinks help to prevent the horse becoming dehydrated and it is essential that the horse drinks as much as possible along the ride*

toughest which is the endurance ride. The rider must keep his own fitness up to the same standard as the horse; also, the way he sits and how he keeps his horse balanced will inevitably influence the performance so it is essential to sit straight – otherwise the horse will be forced to compensate for his unevenness, and this could well cause pressure on the back or elsewhere, and stiffness at some stage. He must be quite sure, too, that his clothing is suitable and is not going to cause any rubs or bruises. Likewise for the horse – everything must be comfortable and in good condition so as to avoid rubs and sores.

The veterinary inspections during any of these rides are tough, and rightly so, but it is very much up to the rider to present the horse in the best possible way. All endurance riders realise how crucial pulse and respiration rates are, and how important it is to build up a picture of the horse's overall progress. By taking the pulse and respiration

● *Despite the rigours of endurance riding this (Ann Newton's) horse looks alert and happy during one of the vet checks. If the fitness build-up has been conscientiously carried out and all goes according to plan on your ride there should be few worries*

rates each week after work at the same place it is easy to see how you are getting on; taking them again after a ten-minute break will also show how quickly the horse is recovering from his work.

With most work it is generally agreed that if the pulse is around seventy-five to eighty after a work session the horse is ready to do some harder training. The pulse and respiration rates should have returned to normal within half-an-hour of a workout. It cannot be overstressed that a gradual building of fitness is essential for the endurance horse, and the horse will certainly not be allowed to continue a competition if the vets consider that pulse and respiration indicate an insufficient level of fitness.

The Hunter

Fitness training for the hunter starts in the same way as for any other horse, with slow work – traditionally on the roads for several weeks. In Britain, hunters come in around the end of July so as to be ready for early cubbing at the end of harvest, usually in early September. Most hunters have the summer out at grass and are turned away early enough to catch the best of the spring grazing; thus they tend to come in grossly fat and are seen walking round the roads often being ridden and led. After such a lay-off it is vital that the horse is given enough time to harden up muscles and tendons and lose excess fat before being asked to work hard.

● *Once the hunter comes in from his summer rest the process of slow conditioning work begins to fitten him for the coming season. Hours of slow road work to strengthen legs and muscles and a reduction in the food intake are necessary to build up fitness. It is important not to do fast work until the horse has lost some weight and is in suitable condition*

At least six weeks are spent at walk and at walk and trot. Once cubbing starts, many owners are keen to make the most of the season and want to go out before their horses are really fit enough. So long as the horse has had a good start, a quiet day's cubbing – which should not usually involve too much fast work at all – will be all right: *but* the rider must be strong-willed enough to stop should this not prove to be the case. All too often one hears of horses suffering strains and injury at the start of the season because their owners could not resist a gallop when hounds had an early run, before the horses were fit. If so, their riders really have only themselves to blame.

Once the hunter has done his slow work and is looking somewhat more svelte, he can do a bit of cantering, usually after about the sixth week. Hill work, if possible, will help to clear his wind, and trotting or cantering up hill always improves overall fitness. A little jumping, too, will help to get horse and rider together and is certainly a good idea. Some people hunt all winter and then do not ride at all during the summer months, and it is important that these hunting riders, most of all, get themselves fit by riding as much as possible – at some stage they should have a school or two over fences to get in tune. A bit of fast work will help to make sure they can still control the horse effectively; this is vital in the hunting field – otherwise you are not only a danger to yourself but to everyone else as well.

Once hunting or cubbing is under way, the hunter does not require a lot of work if he is going out once or twice a week, though he should have steady, slow exercise to maintain fitness. There is a long season ahead so he needs preserving, his legs and back being the most vulnerable areas – saddle sores can easily develop with the rider being in the same position for so long. Look after every cut or sore, cleaning these carefully and allowing them to harden off well. With the hunter it is best to miss one day to allow something to heal properly, rather than being obliged to miss several because you rode him too soon.

The rider must be sympathetic to the horse if he is to enjoy a long season and keep the horse sound. Hunting seems expensive, but if you can enjoy thirty to forty days a season then it is certainly more than worth it and in fact works out quite cheap. Wrecking your horse by doing too much at the start of the winter does, however, make it an extremely expensive sport.

For those who hunt only at weekends the horse may need a canter midweek to keep him clear in his wind; otherwise he should need no more than to hack out quietly in between hunting days. Boots or bandages are usually best left off the hunter, as mud can work its way up underneath and create even more of a problem than if he went without. Most hunters are given a hunter clip which leaves the hair on the legs, and this acts as fairly good protection anyway with the thick winter coat. Make sure shoes are regularly checked as in deep winter going they can quickly get loose.

Keep all tack soft and supple, using Neatsfoot oil if it gets hard, as nothing rubs a horse more than hard leather. As soon as possible after the tack has been taken off the horse wash the mud off well and allow the leather to dry naturally. There are opposing theories as to whether or not to wash the horse and his legs off on return from hunting; personally, I believe both can work well, although if it is really cold perhaps the horse should not be subjected to more water except to sponge off his saddle patch if wet. The old method of rubbing down tired, wet horses with straw is one of the best, stimulating the skin and taking dried mud off at the same time. Straw is also excellent placed round the legs and bandaged on as it still allows air to circulate, and the legs dry quicker like this than with gamgee or Fibagee (cotton sheeting) and bandages. Legs are best bandaged after hunting

● *There are numerous different methods of caring for a horse's legs. A good old-fashioned way of drying off wet or muddy legs is to wrap them with straw and then bandage. Once dry they can be brushed off to remove mud*

following a thorough checkover, whether washed off or not; bandaging keeps the horse warm and increases circulation after the rigours of the day.

Always check your horse's ears. Cold ears to a horse are as uncomfortable as cold feet to a human, and drying and warming these with a towel or by pulling them gently between the palms of your hands will ensure your horse relaxes and settles more quickly. A small nutritious feed or bran mash will be much appreciated, but do not give a huge one if you have had a hard day as a horse may be more vulnerable to colic when he is tired – give his digestive system a chance to get going again.

For riders, it is most important that they take their build-up to hunting fitness as seriously as that of their horses. Ride out as much as possible, do some exercises, jogging, bicycling and so on if you are not fit, and generally look after yourself in the best possible way. Even though hounds rarely run non-stop for long, hunting is still a very strenuous form of riding.

The Polo Pony

Polo is a very ancient and demanding sport, requiring tremendous fitness from both horse and rider. The same basic fitness routine is usual in the early stages, with four to six weeks spent at walk and at walk and trot, and even longer for an animal which has had a leg problem the previous season. Polo ponies are usually several in number and so generally get led in ones and twos. However, it is important that they are ridden in rotation so their backs get hardened up.

Once the basic slow work has been accomplished, the ponies continue to go out hacking but also have some schooling sessions aimed to sharpen up obedience and balance. The pony must be quick and alert to its rider and the ball; it must also be able to stop and turn and gallop very fast in a straight line.

The rider needs to be fit and alert, and must remain in balance at all times despite the speed of the game. The pony must be able to work at maximum effort throughout the chukka (each lasts seven minutes) after which it is usually changed for another. Both horse and rider need to show a high degree of agility, and the horse must be exceptionally quick-footed. Neck-reining is the normal method of steering, as the player's other hand will be holding the polo stick.

● *Learning at an early age makes all sports so much easier. Here the instructor is explaining to his young players how to set about mastering the different manoeuvres required*

The pony must learn from an early age to stop and start quickly, and to turn on the haunches. Control is most important, so suitable bitting is necessary if the pony is strong. Because of the quickness of the game, standing martingales are commonly used and leg protection is essential.

It generally takes about two years to train a polo pony, and it is important that the young pony is given time to adjust physically to the quick turns and sudden changes in pace. Early training is therefore done at walk so that his muscles strengthen gradually and his confidence is built up steadily. Stick and ball training is then introduced, and this *must* be done slowly to start with – a pony will be easily frightened at this stage if the player does not give it time to get accustomed to meeting other players and swinging sticks. It must also learn to 'ride off' and be 'ridden off' with confidence, and to adapt to the sudden changes of balance required as the rider twists and turns in the saddle.

● *Polo in the snow adds to the excitement of this quick and arduous sport. Supreme fitness of horse and rider is vital*

In Britain the polo season is relatively short, beginning at the end of April and finishing in early September. High goal polo usually starts in May and finishes in July. Many of the world's top players then move back to America or elsewhere, to continue playing wherever climatic conditions allow.

To achieve competition fitness, the trainer should allow for two months' minimum preparation: initially, polo ponies must be given serious slow work to harden and strengthen those tendons and muscles which will be taking such stresses and strains in the weeks to come; after about the sixth week they can do a little cantering, with changes of direction being incorporated into their work. A good deal of trotting is useful to start with, then cantering for the month before the first match. As the ponies only walk and canter during their matches, it is vital that they do quite a bit of cantering at this stage; however, they do not need to gallop very often at all, perhaps once a week in a couple of short sharp bursts. It is the slow cantering, the progressive building up of muscle power with schooling and stops and turns, that is essential to the polo pony.

In low goal polo there are four chukkas, in high goal there are six, but as always it is sensible not to overstrain the ponies in the early stages if they are to last out the season.

For the rider it is essential to be very fit for this strenuous game – the very nature of the sport requires quick and sudden changes of direction, and this puts all muscles under severe strain. Seven minutes at speed can seem a very long time, and there is only a short break between chukkas in which to relax. Thus riding fitness, plus any of the stretching and toning exercises, can only be beneficial for the polo player. Make sure you really work at your own fitness at the beginning of the season, and take your pony slowly at first – you should then be able to enjoy a long season, and can certainly be happy in the knowledge that you have prepared yourselves steadily and sensibly for what must be one of the toughest sports in the world.

The Child's Pony

Children's ponies have always been a law unto themselves because inevitably they are used intensively during school holidays, but only as much as time allows during term-time; however, the child's pony is probably the most important mount of all because safety has to be the number one priority. For small children on small ponies fitness is not so important, unless the child is exceptionally competent and is expecting much more than the pony is able to cope with as regards his fitness. However, for the child who wants to do Pony Club activities, to hunt, go to rallies and sponsored rides and to show jump whenever school allows, then there is definitely more of a problem as the pony does need to be fit enough to cope with the demand. Ponies are remarkably versatile and seem to love the variety as much as children, but so often children do not know, care or understand how one activity may affect another, or how strenuous such things are for the pony. Thus it is most important that they are educated at an early stage so that not only do they learn to ride, but they become horsemasters as well. Moreover, all too often parents are not 'horsey' at all, but find themselves the proud owner of a pony with little idea of how to cope other than the fact that it needs feed and water!

Nonetheless, the happy medium has to be found if your child wants to do all these things: the pony must be fit enough to cope with the demands without stress, but still remain calm enough for the child to ride. Ponies are so hardy they will survive most situations, but children must be made to realise that when their ponies are not fit they should *not* gallop about without pause, and that their ponies will get tired so will need a rest *at walk* between periods of effort. They must be taught the basic principles of fitness training, that should be built up *gradually*,

● *The thrill of riding at speed and the concentration, balance and timing required are amply illustrated in this picture taken at the Royal Windsor Horse Show*

● Mounted games are a firm favourite with children. Generally organised by the Pony Club, it is an excellent method of teaching a variety of skills on horseback as well as increasing balance, co-ordination, concentration and timing

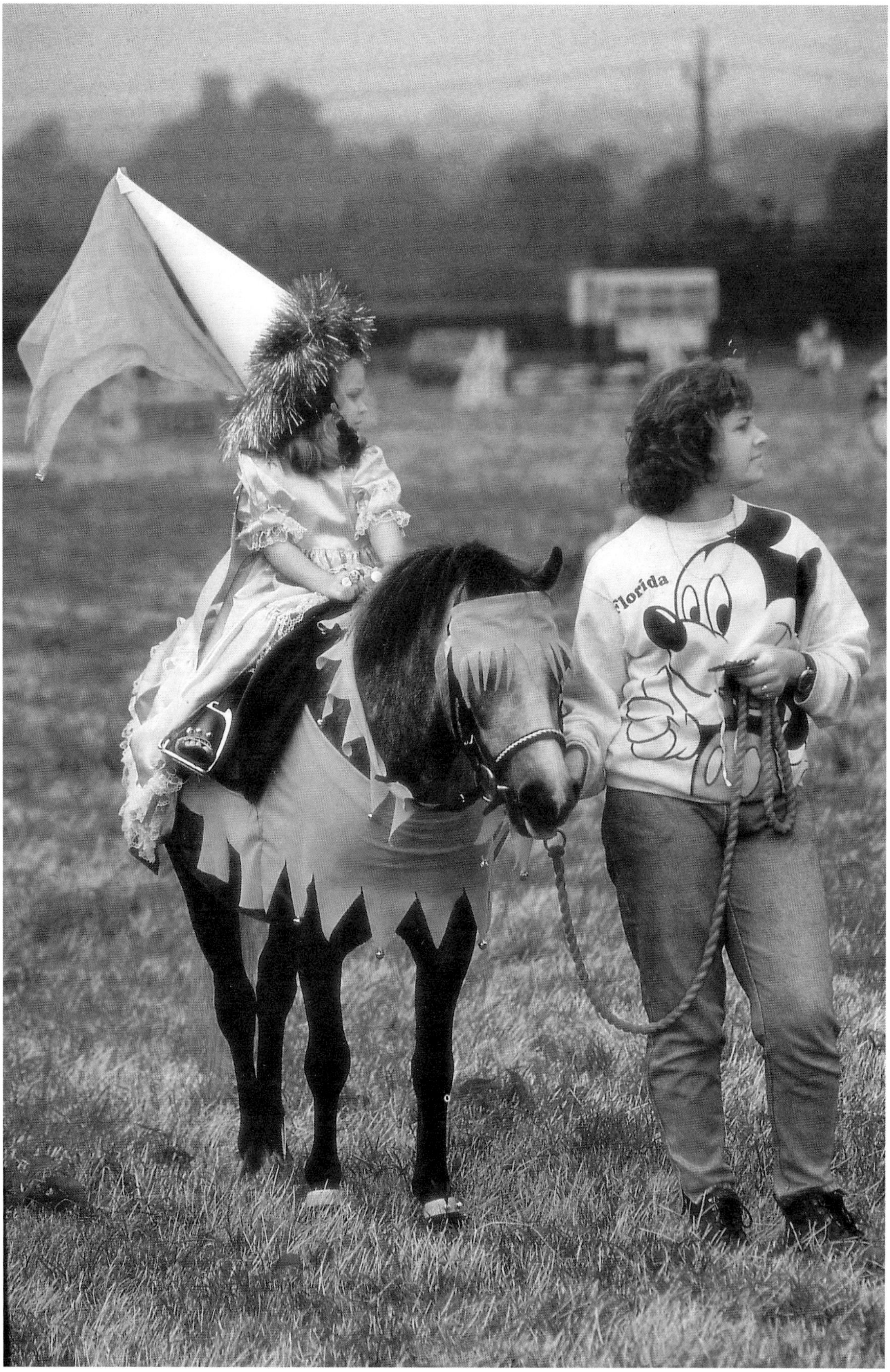
Florida

particularly if the pony is completely unfit, and there should be a strict rule that there is *no* jumping or galloping until the pony is coping with the slower work well. It must be explained to children that tired ponies are much more likely to have accidents and injure themselves if they are not treated properly. Having said all this, make sure riding is fun for them – this is so important for the young.

The best way to get a pony fit is our usual fitness routine: start riding it for a week at walk, for the second week at walk and trot, building up its work day by day. The ideal would be for the child to do this, or the parent if he or she is light enough. If not, sometimes the pony can be led from another horse, though it is a good idea to put a saddle on to help harden up its back; leading it will at least ensure it gets the work to harden legs and tendons and the exercise to prepare it anyway partially for the child. If a pony is getting hot and sweating a lot in his work it is wise to trace clip him so that he doesn't lose too much condition. Make sure his feet are in good shape before he starts work or that he has been shod recently, and watch out for girth galls in the first week or two, or if he is very 'hairy'.

If the fittening methods mentioned above are not possible, a little lungeing at walk and trot only will suffice. Start with five minutes on each rein, and build up so that by the end of the week the pony is doing ten minutes on each rein. Remember to give a little break in the middle. Make the circle as large as possible, and if the pony has not lunged before you will have to train him, quietly repeating your instructions until he obeys your demands. If he is really unfit do *not* canter him on the lunge – this is strenuous work, and more likely to strain him than to do any good.

Gradually build up the work, particularly if he is rather a lazy pony and very fat – starve him a bit if necessary by standing him in the stable or putting him in a paddock with very little grazing. Fat ponies can never

● *Starting to ride at an early age helps to make everything easy. The fancy dress class is fun and gives great incentive to start riding*

● *Children generally love jumping so long as they are confident in their mounts. If the pony is not very fit, make sure it has frequent rests.*
OVERLEAF: *Riding sidesaddle requires the rider to be fit as the position in the saddle makes movement a little awkward*

be fit. The quick, wiry type of pony will soon get fit, and care must be taken with this sort that it doesn't become too much for the child to cope with. Such ponies may be better left out in the field and ridden just once or twice a week, rather than daily. Generally the more you work a pony or horse the fitter it will get, but some keep themselves fairly fit anyway if they are the inquisitive sort and like to take a look at everything that is going on.

As far as the child is concerned, it is always better that the pony is safe and calm than over-fit and unpredictable. You can always stop your child from doing more if the pony is tired, but if the pony is over the top the damage to the child's confidence – if not safety – may already have been done. Never worry, therefore, about whether the pony is fit enough – if it is not, it doesn't matter, as safety must always come first.

The teenager who is experienced and keen should be made to understand what can be

● *The thrill of winning makes everything worthwhile. This show hunter pony winner probably involved a very early start on the day and months of training to achieve success*

expected of the pony for its stage of fitness, and the holiday programme should be organised so that the more strenuous competitions come towards the end of the holidays when the pony is fitter. These older children must learn how to prepare for different events, and should be made to realise the importance of the basic slow fitness work – whoever has actually done it with their pony. The next stage is schooling, or further fittening work in preparation for whatever they are aiming for; but again, care

must be taken that this is not overdone, especially where jumping is concerned – children always want 'just one more go' and must be told, *firmly*, when enough is enough, if only for the ponies' sake!

Make sure tack is safe, and that the child is in control; nothing ruins a child's confidence quicker than to feel the pony is out of control; it will also ruin their hands if they are obliged to yank at a pony's often insensitive mouth. In many cases it is advisable to use a stronger bit – a pelham or a Kimblewick is often ideal – at least until the child has learned to ride with an independent seat, and has good enough co-ordination to use legs and hands correctly.

How to get Involved in the Different Sports

Whatever it is you decide to aim for, there will probably come a time when you will want to become an official member of the club or society affiliated to your chosen sport, and do it on a more serious level. Most sports can be followed in unaffiliated competitions, which provide the chance to learn the ropes and get a feel of what it is all about – but only by taking part in it seriously will you really know how good you are, and what it is you need to concentrate on, because your true standard will only be apparent when you are up against professionals. Most of them will always be willing to help and offer advice, so never be too shy to ask.

By joining the official society or club of your chosen sport you will be sure of receiving all relevant and current information, and

● *Children have a remarkable ability to combine numerous skills on horseback, including long periods of concentration, which is less apparent when involved in other occupations. A sensible, honest pony who is doing its utmost to please its young jockey*

details of the rules that govern it. Once you have taken all this in, you will know what you need to do next, and can then ask the relevant society for advice.

In Britain and America most sports are well established; it is just a matter of getting in touch through the British Horse Society (BHS) or American Horse Shows Association (AHSA) to find out the right body for advice (see Useful Addresses). In most cases horses have to be registered to compete in the more serious competitions, and for this you will have to have an up-to-date flu vaccination certificate for each horse, and maybe other health papers as well. Certain sports require height certificates, which can be arranged through your veterinarian.

You will usually be required to produce membership numbers or registration cards, so it is worth keeping a book with all these details; it is also interesting to keep a record of your outings and results.

Combining Pleasure with Work

Very often it is quite difficult to spend as much time as you would like at your hobby when you have a full-time job, but in most cases people seem to find a way, usually by arranging to be more flexible in their working hours. Even when I was studying as a nurse I managed to get away enough to ride at least three to four times a week, with my family filling in the gaps. While it would be much more difficult nowadays to get as far as the Olympics without a lot of help, there are many who are determined enough to reach quite a high level.

The important thing is to be realistic about your goals, and not to set your sights too high too soon. Take each step sensibly, and if all is going well, move up to the next one. Inevitably there will be ups and downs, and you may have to take longer to re-establish confidence, or work harder to reach a certain level than you had anticipated. You will have to deal with problems as they arise, but as long as you are realistic in your aims and dedicated in your chosen sport, there is no reason why you should not derive a lot of fun, and success, from taking part in it.

● Team chasing is an energetic sport requiring fit riders and horses. It is vital for everyone to remain as close as possible if the team is to achieve a good finishing time

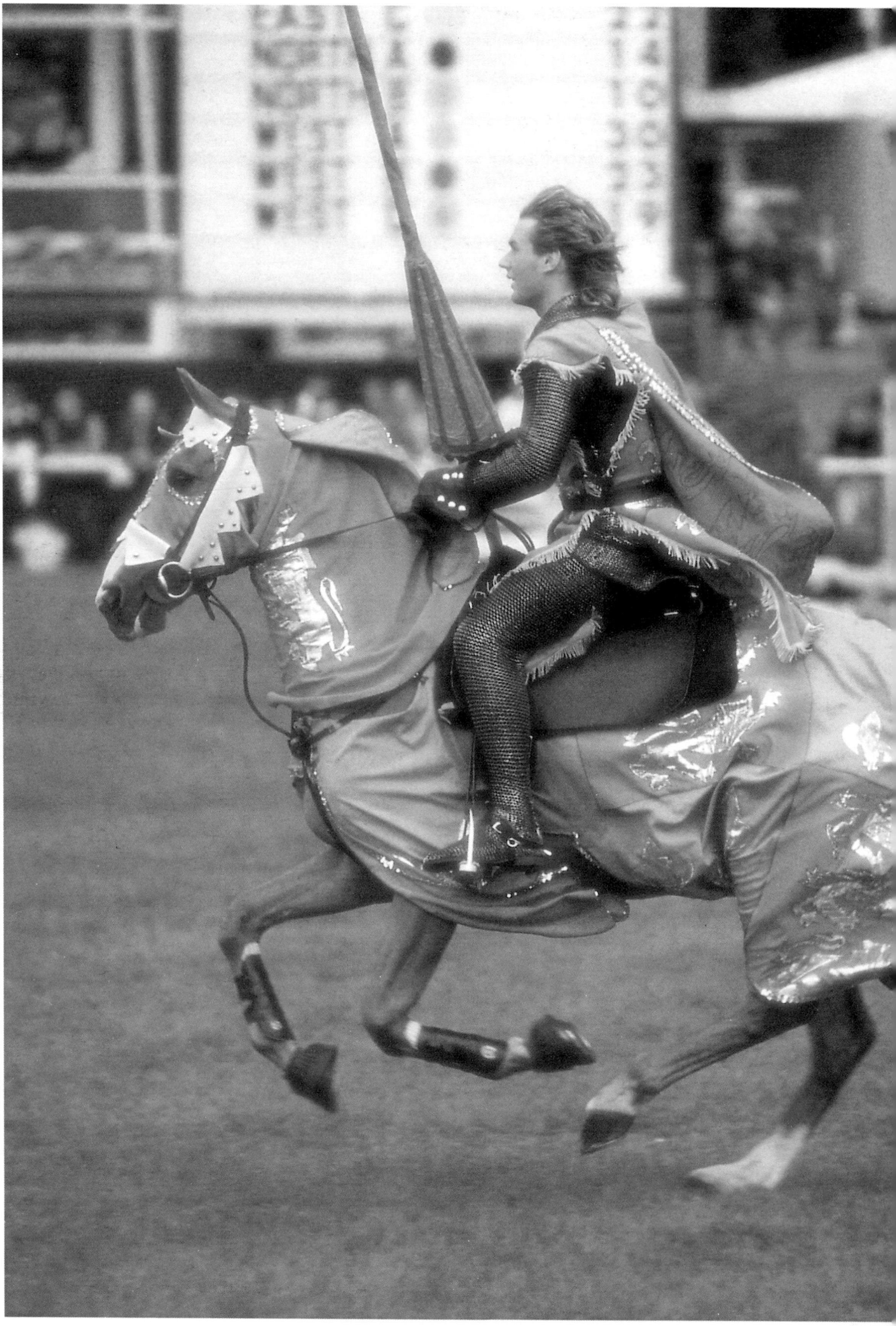

Inevitably there are limits on how far you can or want to go, limits dictated by time, finance, the ability of you or your horse, or for many other reasons – but on the other hand, no one ever knows exactly what can be achieved until they try, and for this reason alone it is well worthwhile to *keep* evaluating the position, and in the light of the progress made to date, deciding what your aims might be for the future. This is exciting – but once it all becomes a chore it loses its appeal, and once you find the fun aspect has gone you are probably best to say 'Enough is enough': so you will always have to keep making decisions. I retired from serious eventing several years ago, but I still get enormous fun from bringing on young horses and then passing them on to talented riders who will take them to the top if they show the right ability. Others which have not seemed right for eventing have gone to other homes where their talents have been employed in different ways.

Whatever you do, remember that to excel at anything both you and the horse must basically enjoy it – otherwise it is simply not worth the effort, the time and the sheer hard work that must be dedicated to training and getting fit. The onus, however, is very much on you, to put in as much as you want to get out of riding horses.

● *Demonstrations of the ancient art of jousting have thrilled thousands. It requires tremendous balance, judgement and co-ordination to be able to gallop at speed towards the opponent carrying the lance*

6 CARE & MANAGEMENT

To achieve maximum health and fitness requires a certain amount of common sense and self-discipline, but generally if you lead a relatively sensible lifestyle, eat, sleep and exercise enough you should not have too many worries. The important factor is to keep everything in perspective and not attempt anything which exceeds your capabilities. Sometimes this is difficult to judge, and is undoubtedly something that comes with experience. For this reason it is always an advantage to have a friend or a trainer who is experienced in your chosen sport and who will be able to give you guidance and advice.

As with most things, if you are confident you achieve far more than if you are worried or unsure. Keep to a routine as much as your lifestyle permits, and allow yourself the time to do what is necessary to achieve your aims. Whenever you come up against a problem *do not* panic, but sit back and work out where things went wrong. You may have to go back a step so as to re-establish confidence at a slightly lower or easier level, before building up again to where you were.

Some people try too hard and put too much into what they are doing, and this can have a depressing effect on both horse and human. 'All work and no play make Jack a dull boy' is in fact a very shrewd saying, because everyone must have a time of relaxation and change if they are to be able to cope with the dedication and work required to succeed. All too often horses are seen going round like robots, their riders looking much the same as if 'over-drilled' – and this is not what is required. Both horse and rider must look happy in their work and have that lightness and enthusiasm which is so pleasing to watch. Variety is essential, so take

care not to become too preoccupied with one problem – do something completely different and come back to it later. This is often the best way, but if you are still having no success get someone to help you; it may well be the *way* you are asking your horse that is not effective or causing him to misunderstand rather than *what* you are asking.

If help is not available you will have to analyse the problem and try to work it out for yourself to see if you can come to some arrangement with your horse. Very often asking for a certain movement slowly in walk will help him understand what is required, and then you can progress from there.

On those occasions when you are too busy to exercise your horse, a day off will not do either of you any harm as long as you remember to cut down his feed. Turn him out or even lead him out if the former is not possible, and give a bran mash or small feed low in protein to prevent the risk of azoturia. Remember not to overwork him the next day, and to give him a really good warming-up period; never do really strenuous work the day after a rest.

Perhaps you have a week's holiday and want to go away: it will be quite all right for the horse to have a break too, provided someone can turn him out or lunge him during that time. If he is greedy be sure to leave instructions to keep his feed down, especially if he is likely to gorge himself on hay or straw, as this will definitely result in an over-large belly on your return.

You may decide instead to concentrate on your riding during this break, in which case plan what you want to do well ahead and make the most of your time either in training or competition work.

First-Aid Tips

Inevitably there are times when the unexpected happens or an injury occurs so it is imperative to have a well-stocked first-aid cupboard containing all the essential items with which to deal with minor injuries. Ideally it should be kitted out for both horse and human, then all that might be required is in the one spot. Make sure everyone knows where the first-aid store is situated and that its contents are kept replenished and clean so that everything is always available.

● *The first-aid kit is an essential part of any stable and should accompany the horse to competitions. Ensure you have poultices, bandages, scissors and antiseptics to cope with emergencies which could arise at any time*

The following list will, I hope, serve as a useful reminder, although everyone will have their own favourites to add.

For the Horse

The vet's telephone number should be clearly displayed.

1 Antiseptic lotion for cleaning wounds
2 Antibacterial spray/powder for application after cleaning
3 Cotton wool for cleaning off wounds, and bowl
4 Gamgee (cotton sheeting)/padding to go under bandages
5 Bandages, stable and/or crêpe to hold dressings in place
6 Scissors (vital for all occasions)
7 Poultices, Animalintex/kaolin
8 Hydrogen peroxide – excellent for cleansing wounds
9 Surgical spirit (rubbing alcohol) for hardening skin
10 Thermometer, for use whenever the horse looks off-colour
11 Stockholm tar for foot injuries
12 Dry non-stick dressings to cover wounds

For the Rider

The ambulance/doctor's telephone number should be clearly displayed.

1 Plasters (Band-Aids), all sizes
2 Tweezers for removing splinters
3 Medical wipes to clean all minor cuts and sores
4 Arnica ointment and pills for bruises
5 Witch hazel for bruises
6 Non-stick dressings
7 Bandage and sling
8 Antiseptic solution for cleaning cuts
9 Cotton wool and bowl
10 Pain killers

Minor Cuts and Scrapes

These need cleaning carefully with a mild antiseptic solution or salt and warm water. Make sure the edges are cleaned properly, and if necessary trim away any hair that may hinder healing. Dry by dabbing gently, then apply either anti-bacterial spray or wound powder as necessary until the injury has healed up.

The Application of Ice

Ice is extremely useful for the treatment of the first stage of severe bruising. By constricting the blood vessels and cooling the painful area it reduces inflammation and brings down swelling, therefore reducing pain. It can be applied in many different ways.

In an emergency the sooner you can get it on the affected area the better, and the bag of frozen peas from the freezer has found favour with many a horse owner during those crucial early hours. Mould the bag of peas round the leg, and bandage lightly in place. Alternative methods can then be used – these include various iced bandages which need half an hour in the freezer before being applied to the legs, and which need replacing every two to three hours; also cold gamgee or special iced leg packs.

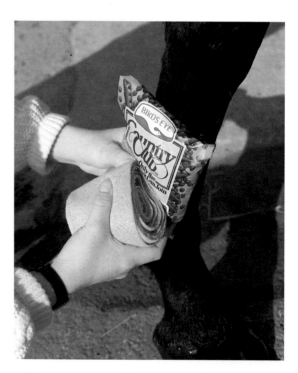

● *In an emergency the sooner you can get something cold (preferably ice) onto a bruise the quicker the bleeding will stop. If all else fails there is likely to be a packet of peas or whatever in the nearest freezer and this makes an excellent ice pack*

You therefore need two ice packs – one in use whilst the previous one is refreezing. Whichever brand you choose, keep replacing the ice for twenty-four to thirty-six hours until the injury has settled and you can start to disperse the bruising within the leg by hot poulticing. Be careful not to cause 'ice burns', which can happen if ice is left in place for too long: either place it over a cloth or piece of cotton to protect the skin, or keep shifting its position so the area does not become affected.

Call your vet whenever there is anything more serious than minor cuts and bruises, and be sure that your horse's tetanus protection is kept up to date. Once it has had its initial inoculations, biannual boosters only are required.

The Kaolin Poultice

Kaolin is used on bruises or filled legs caused by jarring and suchlike, and is a most versatile poultice. It can be used hot or cold and has an excellent soothing effect. Used cold, it will reduce bruising and take the sting out of tired legs that have worked on hard ground; used hot, it is soothing and increases circulation to the legs, helping with inflammation and soft swellings. Once applied, leave in place for twelve to twenty-four hours.

The best way to apply this sort of poultice is to spread the kaolin on a large piece of brown paper (the inside of horse food bags is excellent), cut it to the appropriate size, then apply it to the affected limb(s). Cover with gamgee or other padding, and bandage in place. For a hot poultice, place the kaolin paper in the oven for a couple of minutes, or in the microwave for half a minute. Always test that it is not too hot by placing it on the sensitive part of your palm before applying. To avoid the kaolin sticking to the leg, apply a layer of gauze over your kaolin paper before putting it on the horse. Remove with hot water and a sponge – and this is not always so easy, as kaolin does tend to stick!

The Bran Poultice

Bran can be effectively applied to the feet to draw out bruising. Mix half a scoop of bran

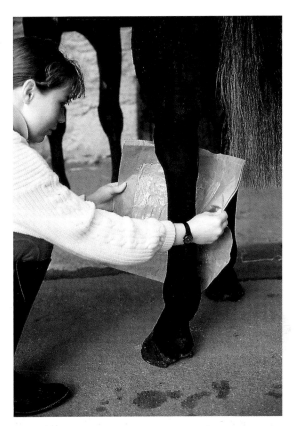

● Kaolin is excellent for poulticing legs. It can be used hot or cold depending on the injury but is not normally put over open wounds. Spread on paper it is easily applied to the affected area. If putting on hot always check the temperature before applying

with boiling water and a tablespoon of Epsom salts; pack this mixture into the sole of the foot, cover with plastic and bandage in place. If available, an Equiboot can be placed on top, as long as it does not cause pressure in vulnerable areas near the bruise.

How to Apply a Poultice

Depending on the type of injury to be treated the first priority must be to clean the wound if there is one. Generally ice is applied to bruises first of all, to stop any bleeding by constricting the superficial blood vessels. Cold water can be trickled over open wounds, but not for too long or at too strong a pressure as this could damage the tissues around the injury. For bruising, trickle cold water for fifteen minutes, three to six times a day.

Once the wound is clean, cut your poultice to the required size and apply it exactly as directed on the packet. *Animalintex* is

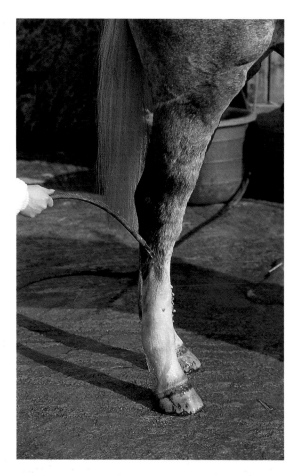

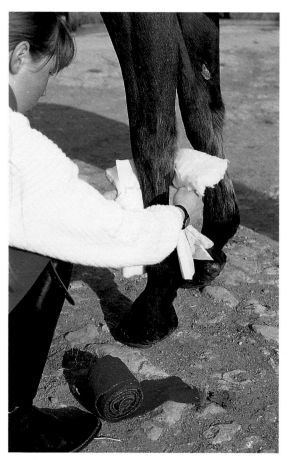

● *Cold hosing every 3 to 4 hours in the early stages following a bad bruise helps to prevent further damage; thereafter hot poulticing to disperse it works well in most cases*

● *The Animalintex poultice is a complete poultice in itself and can be used wet or dry, hot or cold. Follow the instructions on the packet, cover with the enclosed plastic and bandage in position*

the most usual proprietary poultice, and this is used wet or dry, cold or hot: a wet one is more usual, as it will then help to draw any impurities to the surface, an effect which will be enhanced if it is used at blood heat. A cold poultice will also draw, but it is better for wounds that are liable to gape, such as with a tear injury, because it is less likely to open the wound up. Dry poultices have the effect of drying a wound, but they tend to stick which rather defeats their purpose.

Tendon Injuries

A tendon sprain or strain is the one really serious injury every rider dreads. Normally there is heat, and sometimes swelling in the affected leg and the horse is usually lame. The onset of symptoms may be sudden or gradual, but in all cases it will require a long rest to recover, and this could mean anything from weeks to a year. The immediate treatment is to apply ice to the suspected area, and keep the horse quiet. Call the vet straightaway, as early initial treatment can help to reduce further damage – occasionally one's worst fears turn out to be no more than bruising, and once this has disappeared the horse can continue in work.

Puncture Wounds

Deep puncture wounds can be dangerous, as dirt tends to get right inside causing infection – it is better if they bleed freely as this does help to clear out the wound. However, very often these injuries do not bleed in this way, so call your vet as he may need to prescribe an antibiotic.

Illness and Disease

Taking a temperature has already been discussed, but always take the horse's temperature if he looks ill or is not eating. if he does have a raised reading – above 39.5°C (103°F) – always call the vet, as he may have a virus or be in pain. If possible isolate the sick horse or move others away.

Colic

Colic is the term used for abdominal pain, regardless of the cause. The horse will indicate his discomfort by restlessness, looking round and/or kicking at his stomach, and will probably try to roll in his efforts to relieve the pain. He will have a raised pulse and respiration rate, as well as temperature if the pain is severe; he may also break out in sweating patches.

Call the vet immediately, and keep the horse up on his feet and quietly walking. Many vets do not advocate continuous walking which was the normal treatment for colic, but nevertheless keep the horse quietly occupied and do not let it roll; this may cause a twisting of the gut which could prove fatal.

Laminitis

This is an extremely painful condition of the feet, caused by the inflammation of the sensitive laminae in the feet; it is so highly stressful because the hoof wall cannot expand to accommodate the inflammation. The horse will quickly show classic symptoms of this condition: he will lean back from his front feet with his hind feet tucked underneath, trying to take the pressure off his front toes by putting his weight on his heels. He will be very reluctant to move, and his temperature, pulse and respiration rates will probably be raised.

● *The typical stance of a horse with laminitis (inflammation of the laminae in the feet). Because the foot wall cannot expand this condition is extremely painful and thought to be caused by diet changes*

There are generally two types of laminitis, acute and chronic. Acute laminitis comes on very suddenly and can be caused by a sudden change in the diet or grass; and chronic laminitis is when the horse has had the condition for some time, resulting in rotation of the pedal bone because of the increasing pressures within the foot. This leaves the distinctive rings in the growth of the outside wall of the hooves. The condition is particularly common in small, overfat ponies but it can affect all horses and is thought to be associated with diet. Bran mashes and Epsom salts, and symptomatic relief of pain in the feet by cold hosing will help. Always keep ponies away from very lush grass, as this can precipitate the condition.

● *If medicine is not given in the feed or by injection it can be mixed with water and put into the mouth via a syringe (without the needle!). This is very useful for the horse who is a sensitive feeder and dislikes any form of additive*

Administering Medicine

Most powders or medicines are given by mixing them in well with the horse's feed, which should always be dampened so that it does not stay stuck to the side of the manger or feed bowl. Some horses do not like the taste, however, and refuse to eat; so if you do not have success this way, powders can be mixed with a little water in a 10–20ml syringe (*without* the needle!) and then administered by placing it up into the mouth and squirting gently upwards. Keep your fingers over the end until you have it in position.

Thrush

This is a condition of the foot in which the frog becomes soggy and foul-smelling. The feet must be kept clean and dry, and any soft bits of frog should be trimmed off and the frog dried up with antibiotic spray. Spray twice daily until the condition clears up; it is often associated with dirty bedding, so check your stable management. Stockholm tar applied to the feet is also useful in treating this condition. In bad cases the horse will go lame.

Ringworm

Ringworm is a highly contagious fungal condition of the skin. There are several different varieties, but in all cases the hair comes off in patches, usually circular, leaving a moist scaly area. Treatments include 'washes' with antifungal action, in-feed powders, or sprays to be used on the affected areas. Keep the horse isolated, and try to keep *all* equipment – grooming kit, tack and so on – separate from that used by others. Once the condition has subsided, usually after the hair has started to grow again over the patches, disinfect everything thoroughly.

Basic Care During an Outing

The horse will perform to a higher standard if you are able to make an outing as easy as possible for him. Travel stress does exist, and the build-up associated with going to an event, whether large or small, needs careful management.

Try to change your routine as little as possible before, during and after your journey, and in particular stick to feeding times. Do not excite your horse unnecessarily with a lot of 'preparation'; certainly he will need to be looking clean and tidy, but any trimming up and washing of manes and tails is best

● *A horse correctly dressed for travelling*

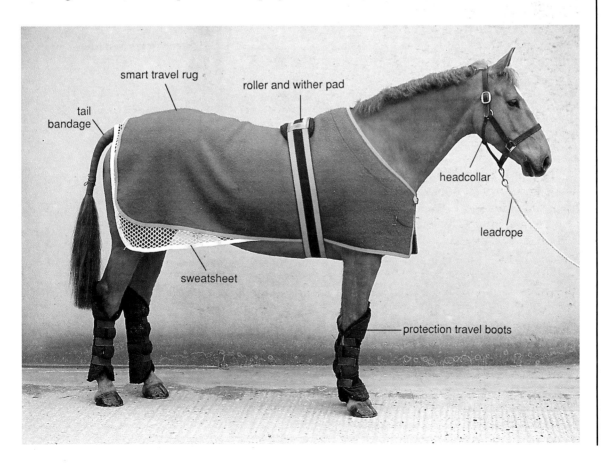

smart travel rug

roller and wither pad

tail bandage

headcollar

leadrope

sweatsheet

protection travel boots

● *Prepare everthing carefully and methodically before travelling. Some people have their own stable or horse colours which can look very smart. Keep your travelling kit clean and tidy at all times, in readiness for the next outing*

done two or three days before so that the horse does not start to associate such efforts with an outing. Greys, of course, are not so easy and usually require a major clean an hour before you leave!

Prepare everything for your journey and take water, hay and feed with you. Be sure your horse is adequately protected for the journey – how much depends on your travelling vehicle, but bandages or travelling boots, adequate rugs, a poll protector to prevent injury to the head when loading if the box or trailer is low, and a tail guard would be advisable; and then your tack, studs, grooming kit, first-aid kit and your own clothes must all be squeezed in somewhere. Try to be methodical in your packing and get into a routine so that you always put everything in the same place; you will then be able to see if you have forgotten something,

too hot – and that he is relaxed. Never leave him alone at a competition unless you are satisfied that he is settled; young horses in particular can be excitable and unpredictable, especially if you take two horses and then remove one of them. Always have someone there to help if you think this situation might arise.

Never leave the horse standing for hours with its tack, boots or bandages on as legs and back are liable to sweat under these and be uncomfortable. Nor should large studs be left in for long periods, unless there is a thick layer of bedding or rubberised floor they can sink into; on a hard surface they will seriously unbalance the foot.

If your horse has worked hard or galloped, make sure he has had plenty of walking and time to settle down before he is loaded up to come home. Always offer him a drink, and let him relax and travel home with hay to pick at. Check him over on arrival and change his rugs if necessary. Many people leave bandages on overnight after an outing, as extra warmth which increases circulation to the area. Give a small feed on your return, then leave the horse in peace to rest. Check him later before leaving him for the night.

The following day bandages should be removed and the horse thoroughly checked over. If necessary wash his legs to remove any mud or sweat which might have accumulated and check his heels. Give him a good grooming to remove sweat and either lead him out or turn him out.

Horses that live out anyway can be turned straight out, as long as they have not got hot travelling. If they have, they may need a New Zealand rug on once they have cooled off a bit unless it is midsummer and warm enough; give them a feed out in the field. Check them carefully the next day – they should be inspected thoroughly all over and dry sweat brushed off well. A day off would be a nice reward, or at least an easy day after the exertions of the previous day.

Sort out all your kit, clean it and tidy it away for the next time, remembering to make a note of anything you should have taken that was not included. Clean out the trailer or horsebox well so that it can air properly and the floor have a chance to dry.

and will always know where to find each item. Always allow ample time to get there, and drive considerately so that your horse is not jolted around too much and arrives in a calm and relaxed state.

On arrival, find out when and where you are competing; look at courses or whatever needs to be done, and then plan your day. Give any helpers their instructions; take the haynet away if necessary; offer a drink if hot; and sort out your kit.

During the day, check your horse for warmth – is he warm enough, or not getting

Fitness Aids for Horses

In this scientific age there are an increasing number of weird and wonderful gadgets that can be used as an aid to fitness – some good, most very expensive and some really not accessible at all – but all are worth knowing about in case you find you have the opportunity to use one. They include horse walkers, equine swimming pools and treadmills, and they all have a place depending on your aims; if available, they may well prove a real bonus.

Horse walkers are probably the most common and can now be found in many stables both large and small. They are no substitute

● *Horse walkers are common in most big yards and racing stables and enable the horse to have regular exercise or a warm-up period before and/or after being ridden. The larger the model the better for the horse who should not turn in small circles for too long*

for ridden work, but they do enable a busy yard to get the horses out of the stable and walking, and even jogging with some models. The horse needs to be introduced quietly to the walker; he should be led round in it for the first few times until he understands that it is mechanically operated and gets used to the nudging if he does not move. Most models accommodate from two to six horses. The small models, however, require the horse to move on quite a small circle so the direction must be changed fairly frequently to prevent the horse developing more on one side than the other. Most horses quickly adapt to this way of exercise. It is an excellent way of being sure the horse has moved about and that his circulation has been adequately stimulated before more strenuous work takes place.

For the permanently stabled horse that does not get a chance to go out in the field, horse walkers can be a welcome change

from being cooped up in a box for twenty-three hours. A morning session before proper work commences and if necessary a cooling off period as well, and then twenty minutes or so in the afternoon, enable a busy rider to cope with more horses. It also means the horse is assured of an excellent build-up before his work and a chance to wind down afterwards, as well as a relaxed walk in the afternoon.

Swimming pools are very popular, particularly in the racing world, and are extremely useful for working a fit horse whilst not jarring his legs. They *must*, however, be used sensibly as swimming is very strenuous for the horse – it is easy to overdo things in the early stages unless precautions are taken.

Introduce the horse to swimming gradually: one or two minutes is ample for the first time; then bring him out, and once his heart and breathing have returned to normal, repeat the session. It is most important that the horse breathes normally during swimming so that he does not become exhausted – short sessions are essential to start with, whilst he learns to adapt to this new experience.

Swimming should never replace proper work, but it does have a useful place in the fitness programme of horses with leg problems and suchlike. Some pools are straight, others round; in the latter it is important to work in both directions for even muscle development.

There are various adaptations based on the swimming pool, including water treadmills. And of course if you happen to live near the sea, the most effective and natural alternative is to ride through the water at knee height, quite apart from being a wonderful experience; the horse will be working hard as the pressure of the water is exerted against his legs and will have to use his muscles more because he has to pick them up higher to get through the water. Salt water has a beneficial effect on the legs, too, with its cooling and drawing properties.

Treadmills enable the horse to work with a minimum of concussion. Most can be tilted to simulate hill work, and the speed can be

● *Swimming has long been popular with competition riders once the horse has finished his basic fitness work. Always introduce the horse to swimming gradually, and don't expect him to go for too long in one go. It is excellent for making a horse 'blow' without putting strain on the legs*

altered to suit the horse's paces, and set to go as fast or slow as is comfortable for him. Care must be taken to introduce a horse gradually so that he is not frightened. Popular in America and Australia, treadmills are now to be found in several racing and competition yards in Britain, and in rehabilitation centres where their use is general.

While any of the above can be extremely useful, it must be stressed that none is a substitute for ridden work, which is the only way to develop muscle and power in a day by day training routine. However, this will only be the case if the horse is worked correctly, so that his muscles are developing in the right way. Just as with your own fitness, he will only improve if worked steadily and progressively towards an ultimate goal.

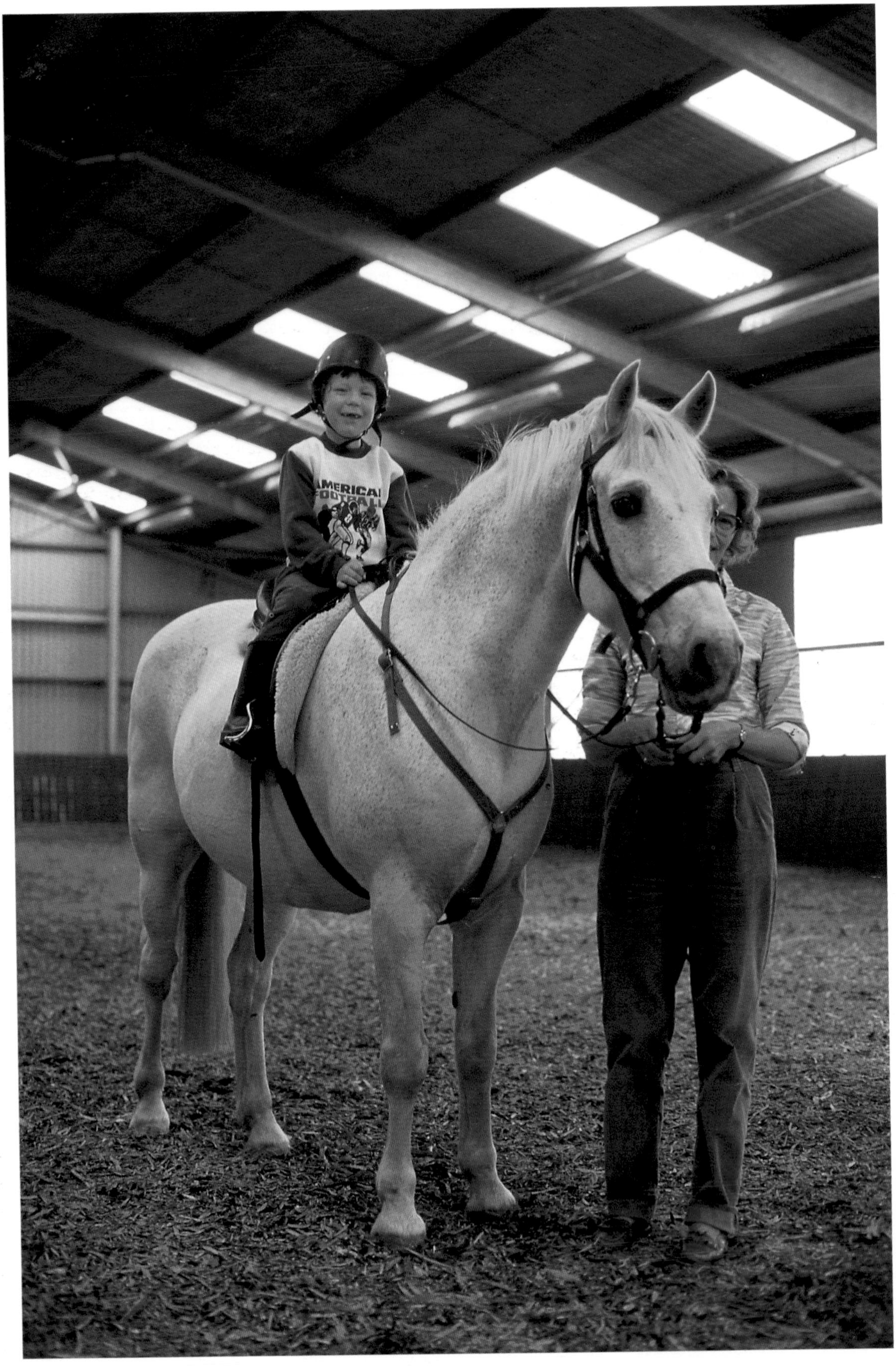

Riding as Therapy

Handicapped as we all are today by the pressure of modern technology, any means of getting fit to help us regain lost condition must surely be considered therapeutic. Years ago the horse kept us fit: we used him as public transport whenever it was necessary or desirable to venture beyond walking distance, and of course with no telephone and no television that occurred far more often than today – in terms of entertainment and communication with others, we had to get up and go. Today we seldom need to bother, and if we do there is always the car or some form of mechanised transport to convey us. Thus what we are saying is that the very animal for which we wish to get ourselves into condition is in fact the one which in many instances is most able to help us!

Of course in the pursuit of fitness individual needs may vary enormously: at one extreme there is the dedicated rider whose physical fitness leaves little to be desired; at the other there is the person who, for some inborn or accidentally acquired reason, must contend with actual physical disabilities. However, few of us are without some handicap, either physical, mental or emotional.

Sadly it has become the custom in modern-day society to put people into convenient categories. For instance a person with only one arm, or even with only partial use of it, is usually designated as 'handicapped'

● *For those confined to a wheelchair the opportunity to be up on a horse is a unique and exhilarating experience. The movement of the horse is well known to help many suffering from a variety of disabilities and is a tremendous boost to confidence and self-esteem*

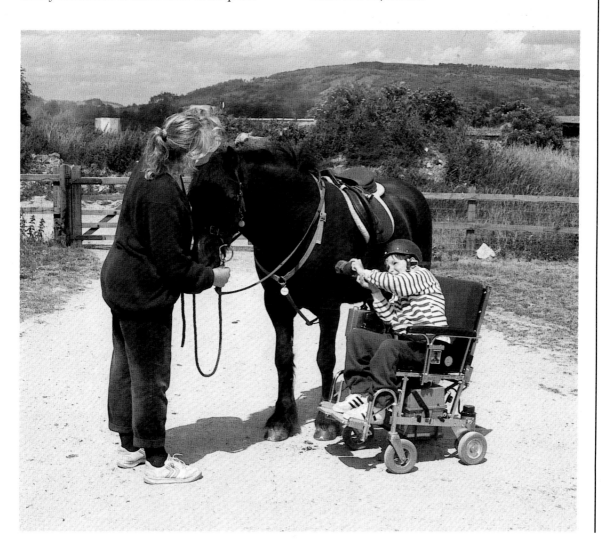

whereas another with poor sight is fortunate enough to go unclassified! On consideration this is a sad state of affairs, since all of us with less-than-perfect sight know that without our glasses we are undoubtedly considerably more handicapped than someone who takes it as a matter of course to operate with only one hand!

Similar comparisons can be drawn in terms of the intellect and emotions. Who can really say at what level a person becomes 'handicapped' within the enormous range of intelligence to be found in any random group of people? Without doubt most of us would appear to be fairly limited if we were compared with, say, Einstein! On the other hand, the children at the top end of one of our special schools for those with learning

● *It is very useful to be able to practise basic techniques of vaulting on the vaulting barrel before doing similar exercises on the horse. The Fortune Centre of Riding Therapy specialises in helping horse-motivated people with particular special needs to fully benefit from their therapeutic teaching with horses*

difficulties, are often not visibly handicapped when compared with the ordinary man in the street. And why, we ask, is it acceptable practice for someone with a psychiatric diagnosis whose behaviour is perfectly sensible and socially acceptable with medication, to be categorised as less normal than a neurotic woman whose behaviour is driving her entire family to distraction?

Thus we might conclude that we can all do with some sort of therapy: and this comes in many forms – it is a matter of each to his own. For some it may be music, painting or dance; for some football, swimming or jogging; for yet others a computer, or tinkering with machinery. Gardening is therapeutic to many people. The answer is that an effective therapy is whatever *motivates* the individual; if you have read this far, then presumably horses are for you, or at least for those you are setting out to help.

Horses can be therapeutic in three main ways: they can stimulate their riders physically, mentally and emotionally, and for most of us they work in any one or more

combinations of these three ways. In order to have the desired effect there are, of course, a number of different activities which can be used. It is common practice in the field of riding therapy to divide the work of the horse into three categories: educational and psychological riding; hippotherapy; and sport riding.

Educational and Psychological Riding

This is when the horse is used to enhance the individual's ability to learn. It is now understood that a child who loves horses is often able to acquire, in their company, knowledge of things that he or she may previously have found difficult. Just as swimming and other sports are part of the curriculum in most schools, so it is becoming more acceptable to use horses as a desirable medium for learning. Videos have been made of educational exercises demonstrating how to teach such basic things as reading and simple mathematics through horses, and numerous articles have been written to illustrate instances where this might be advantageous and advisable.

There are two basic reasons why people might fail to learn: either some straightforward specific learning problem is the cause of the trouble; or/and an emotional disturbance occurs, which interferes with a person's learning processes. In both cases if horse motivation is present, natural relaxation occurs – and it cannot be stressed strongly enough the importance of this factor if therapy is to succeed – and this relaxed state allows the mind and feelings to soak up positive messages rather than to remain in their previous fixed and negative condition. It is obvious to see in this the very close connection which exists between mind and body.

Hippotherapy

This is a term which has caused a certain amount of confusion, and for some it is perhaps easier to think instead of 'Physiotherapy on horseback'. Apart from the pig, the horse is the animal that moves most closely to the human being when it is walking – it is a lateral mover, and the walk is a four-beat pace.

This means that the rider placed correctly on the horse's back has one side of the body swung forward first, followed immediately by the other; thus without any conscious effort on the rider's part, a horse that moves well and is properly handled either by the rider himself or where necessary by a therapist, naturally encourages correct body movement. Careful investigation has shown that a horse walks comfortably at seventy-five steps per minute, which translates into over two thousand per half-hour; this means that in that time, there are over one thousand opportunities to practise straightening on one side of the body alone.

This is a very straightforward way of looking at the meaning of hippotherapy, and in fact there is much more to it than that – for example the warmth of the horse's back is also of great value. For any rider, whether he is in need of extensive help to relax, as in a case of hemiplegia, or is simply stiff from age, lack of practice or for some other simple reason – sitting on a moving horse, preferably on just a sheepskin and doing nothing other than remaining centred and erect and allowing himself to be moved by the horse, will do wonders in a very short time. Moreover this physical approach encourages relaxation of the mind, since a relaxed body means a relaxed mind; thus it also means, of course, a more receptive brain to deal with input of information. All riders can try this out for themselves if they are not already aware of it: when you are particularly stressed and thus tense, sit on a quiet but free-moving horse in walk, and allow it to carry you. Be passive but correct, and *do not try to enforce your will.* Very quickly you will feel the stress signals retreating and experience a sensation of deep relaxation.

Sport Riding

This is a term used amongst practising riding therapists to emphasise the therapeutic value of riding for its own sake. Thus it is not always necessary to concentrate on either educational or physical therapy in order for the horse to do his work, and many would consider there is nothing much more

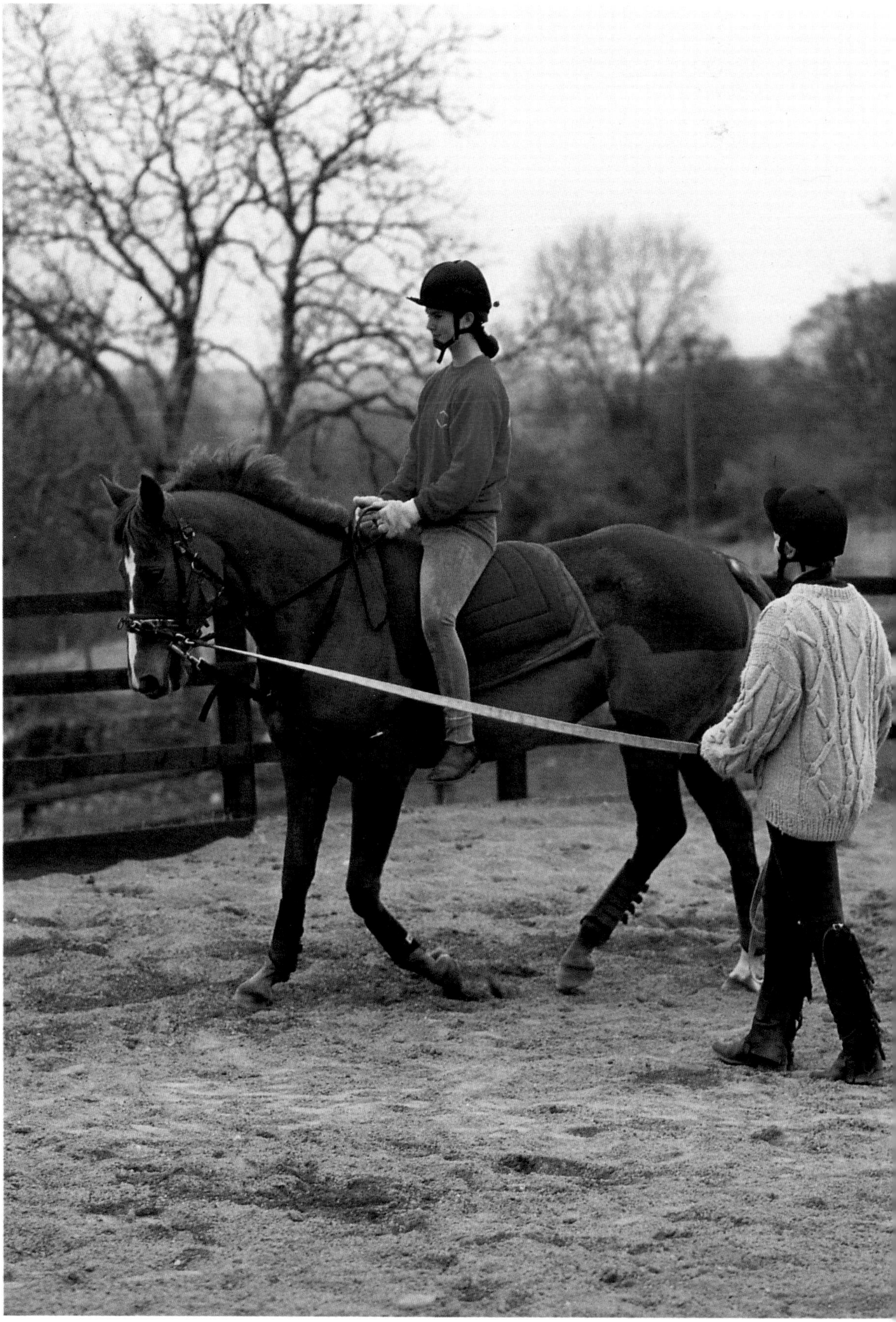

therapeutic to both the mind and body than the sheer pleasure of simply riding a horse. This can apply to all sorts and conditions of people, as long as they have a natural affinity with horses and enjoy riding. However, if they would rather sit in a car or on a bicycle and the idea of riding a horse is threatening to them in any way, then riding therapy, even through sport, is not for them. It is perhaps worth mentioning here that there are occasional exceptions, in particular those people who actually need a challenge that may in the first instance fill them with some apprehension. Such cases need very special handling and as always, when talking of horses, meticulous attention must be paid to safety at all times and in every situation.

As in educational riding and hippotherapy, sport riding can be therapeutic to the whole spectrum of the horse world. There is certainly no denying that to the average rider hunting – simply riding through the countryside for pure pleasure – or competing at whatever level, is by definition very therapeutic. Fifty years ago most people would not have considered it appropriate for heavily handicapped individuals to ride horses at all, let alone to compete; but thanks to the establishment and work of organisations throughout the world dedicated to this, the situation has changed radically.

● *Hippotherapy is the use of the moving horse to aid posture as far as possible and thereby improve a person's physical condition. This is most readily achieved by the use of a pad on the horse's back, which not only enables closer contact than a saddle but allows the warmth of the horse's body to get through to that of the rider, therefore encouraging quicker relaxation which must precede any improvement in condition. It is essentially at the walk that this work takes place and should not be confused with 'learning to ride'*

CONCLUSION

The intention of this book has been to guide the rider to maximum enjoyment of a chosen sport through helpful and practical advice on how things can be achieved, even if he is unable to ride full time. There are still many successful competitors who are amateur in the true sense of the word, able to compete at the top having set out to achieve their ambitions and succeeded.

For all, however, fitness plays a major part in their success and although it is seldom necessary to do really strenuous workouts or run for miles, it is vital for every horse and rider to be sufficiently fit if they are going to compete amongst the rest in the best possible conditions.

I hope this book will encourage many people to the view that riding and competing is quite possible with a little careful planning and preparation, and that you do not have to suffer to be able to do so – Keep Fit and Good Luck!

ACKNOWLEDGEMENTS

I would like to thank the many people who helped in so many ways towards the publishing of this book, and in particular Sandra McCallum, for typing the manuscript from almost illegible handwritten notes; Bob Langrish for his time and care over the photographs; Sue Hall for her understanding and patience throughout. Thanks are also due to Dr Peter Cronau, Diane Bell, Lorraine Walker, Kristin Kosowan, Darrell Scaife, Sue Green, Lucinda Stockley, Lisa Harrowsmith, Nadine Ronan and Franziska Lewinski.

I am indebted to Mrs Yvonne Nelson for her contribution on therapeutic riding, and to the staff and students at the Fortune Centre of Riding Therapy who were such an inspiration towards the writing of this book.

USEFUL ADDRESSES

Further Information

For those people not able to own their own horses, or for whom attending a conventional riding school would be ill-advised, there are still opportunities to ride. In England there are various establishments where help can be obtained, and which offer courses in educational and psychological riding therapy, both on a residential and non-residential basis. Hippotherapy and sport riding for the disabled is available in many areas and overseas.

UK

British Horse Society, British Equestrian Centre, Stoneleigh, Kenilworth, Warwickshire CV8 2LR

British Show Jumping Association, British Equestrian Centre, Stoneleigh, Kenilworth, Warwickshire CV8 2LR

British Show Pony Society, 124 Green End Road, Sawtry, Huntingdon, Cambridgeshire PE17 5XA

British Vaulting Association, Gwanas Fawr, Dolgellau, Gwynedd

Endurance Riding Group, British Equestrian Centre, Stoneleigh, Kenilworth, Warwickshire CV8 2LR

Fortune Centre of Riding Therapy, Avon Tyrell, Bransgore, Christchurch, Dorset BH23 8EE

Hurlingham Polo Association, Ambersham Farm, Midhurst, West Sussex GU29 0BX

Pony Club, British Equestrian Centre, Stoneleigh, Kenilworth, Warwickshire CV8 2LR

Riding for the Disabled, Avenue R., National Agricultural Centre, Kenilworth, Warwickshire CV8 2LY

NORTH AMERICA
American Endurance Ride Conference, 701 High St, #203, Auburn, CA 95603-4727

American Horse Council, 1700 K St, NW, Suite 300, Washington, DC 20006-3805

American Horse Shows Association, Inc, 220 East 42nd St, #409, New York, NY 10017-5876

American Riding Instructor Certification Program, PO Box 282, Alton Bay, NH 03810-0282

American Vaulting Association, PO Box 3663, Saratoga, CA 95070-1663

National 4-H Council, 7100 Connecticut Ave, Chevy Chase, MD 20815-4999

North American Riding for the Handicapped Association, PO Box 33150, Denver, CO 80233

United States Combined Training Association, 461 Boston Rd, #D6, Topsfield, MA 01983-1295

United States Dressage Federation, PO Box 80668, Lincoln, NE 68501-0668

United States Pony Clubs, 4071 Iron
Works Pike, Lexington, KY 40511

United States Vaulting Federation,
RD 1, Box 235, Pittstown,
NJ 08867-9722

AUSTRALIA
Arabian Horse Society of Australia Ltd,
226 George Street, Windsor, NSW 2756

Australian Pony Stud Book Society,
Showground, Paddington, NSW 2021

Australian Quarter Horse Association,
91 Kable Ave, Tamworth, NSW 2340

Australian Saddle Pony Association Ltd,
RASS/grnds, Drive Ave, Paddington,
NSW 2012

Australian Stock Horse Society Ltd,
92 Kelly St, Scone, NSW 2337

Australian Trainers Association,
1 Queens Road, Melbourne, Vic 3004

Pony Club Association of Queensland Inc,
11 Constance Street, Fortitude Valley,
Qld 4006

Pony Club Association of South Australia,
Recreation & Sports Admin, 1 Sturt St,
Adelaide SA 5000

Pony Club Association of Victoria Inc, 12
Warleigh Grove, North Brighton, Vic 3186

Pony Club Association of Western
Australia, State Equestrian Centre,
Brigadoon, WA 6056

Pony Riding for the Disabled Association,
McIntyre Ctr, Pinjara Hills, Qld 4069

Queensland Quarter Horse Association,
PO Box 351, Rockhampton, Qld 4700

Riverina Quarter Horse Association Inc,
PO Box 153, South Wagga Wagga, NSW
2650

South Tasmanian Quarter Horse
Association, Boonderoo, Brinkmans Road,
Glenlusk, Tas 7012

Tasmanian Quarter Horse Association,
Midlands Highway, Mangalore, Tas 7030

Thoroughbred Racehorse Owners
Association, 416 St Kilda Road, Melbourne,
Vic 3004

INDEX

Entries in *italics* indicate illustrations